MYTHOLOGY

Edith Hamilton

AUTHORED by Stephen Haskell
UPDATED AND REVISED by Adam Kissel

COVER DESIGN by Table XI Partners LLC
COVER PHOTO by Olivia Verma and © 2005 GradeSaver, LLC

BOOK DESIGN by Table XI Partners LLC

Published by GradeSaver LLC, www.gradesaver.com

First published in the United States of America by GradeSaver LLC. 2008

GRADESAVER, the GradeSaver logo and the phrase "Getting you the grade
since 1999" are registered trademarks of GradeSaver, LLC

ISBN 978-1-60259-128-8

Printed in the United States of America

For other products and additional information please visit
http://www.gradesaver.com

Table of Contents

Biography of Hamilton, Edith (1868-1963)..1

About Mythology...3

Character List..5

Major Themes..15

Glossary of Terms...19

Short Summary..21

Summary and Analysis of Persephone; Dionysus (Bacchus)............................25

Summary and Analysis of The Creation of the Earth......................................29

Summary and Analysis of Prometheus; Pandora; Prometheus and Io..............31

Summary and Analysis of Europa; the Cyclops Polyphemus..........................35

Summary and Analysis of Narcissus; Hyacinth; Adonis................................37

Summary and Analysis of Cupid and Psyche...41

Summary and Analysis of Pyramus and Thisbe; Orpheus and Eurydice;
  Ceyx and Alcyone; Pygmalion and Galetea..45

Summary and Analysis of Baucis and Philemon; Endymion; Daphne;
  Alpheus and Arethusa..49

Summary and Analysis of Phaethon; Pegasus and Bellerophon......................53

Summary and Analysis of Otus and Ephialtes; Daedalus..............................57

Summary and Analysis of Perseus...59

Summary and Analysis of Theseus...63

Summary and Analysis of Hercules; Atalanta..65

Summary and Analysis of The Quest for the Golden Fleece...........................67

Table of Contents

Summary and Analysis of Tantalus and Niobe; Iphigenia Among the Taurians..69

Summary and Analysis of Oedipus; Antigone.....................................71

Suggested Essay Questions..73

What Is True about a Myth?...77

Author of ClassicNote and Sources..79

Quiz 1...81

Quiz 1 Answer Key...87

Quiz 2...89

Quiz 2 Answer Key...95

Quiz 3...97

Quiz 3 Answer Key...103

Quiz 4...105

Quiz 4 Answer Key...111

Biography of Hamilton, Edith (1868-1963)

Edith Hamilton was a pioneering female educator and writer on mythology. Born in Germany and raised in Indiana, she excelled in academia from a very early age. As a young child, Hamilton learned Latin, Greek, French, and German. She attended Miss Porter's school in Connecticut until her father's business went bankrupt. At that point, she and her sisters taught themselves.

Edith proceeded to college at Bryn Mawr in Pennsylvania. In 1895, she became the first woman to study at the University of Munich in Germany. With this strong education, Hamilton became the headmistress of Bryn Mawr Preparatory School for Girls in Baltimore, Maryland, in 1896. She was only twenty-nine years old.

After a remarkable twenty-six-year career, Hamilton retired from education in 1922. But she did not stop working. She moved to New York City with her life partner, Doris Fielding Reid, and began a career writing scholarly articles on Greek drama and myths. Between 1930 and 1957, Hamilton published books and articles that to this day are considered defining analyses of ancient literature, culture, and life.

Her writing took off with The Greek Way, written in 1930, which compared life in ancient Greece to that in modern Greece. Hamilton followed up by writing The Roman Way, which explored similar themes in Roman life. The Prophets of Israel, Three Greek Plays, Mythology, and The Golden Age of Greek Literature all marked the significant success of her prolific career.

In her elder years, people around the world praised Hamilton for her groundbreaking role as a female academic. President John F. Kennedy invited her to his inauguration. She was elected to the American Academy of Arts and Letters. But most significant to Hamilton, at the age of 90, she traveled to Greece for the first time, where the city of Athens made her an honorary citizen.

Hamilton died in 1963 at the age of 95 in Washington, DC. Her rich life and her impressive body of written work still inspire students and academics alike.

About Mythology

Mythology is perhaps the most highly acclaimed modern collection of Greek and Roman (and even some Norse) myths. Written by Edith Hamilton in 1942, the collection draws on classical and other ancient sources to retell a wide variety of tales. In her introduction, Hamilton admits the difficulty of compiling stories that have been passed down by thousands of writers for thousands of years.

Greek mythology, like other mythologies, illustrates the origins of the world and the adventures of the gods, heroes, and mythological creatures who recur throughout the tales. Originally, the stories were passed down through oral tradition, though eventually they were written in various texts. The oldest literary sources for many myths are Homer's *Iliad* and *Odyssey*, which probably originated in oral traditions themselves, as well as the *Theogony* and the [Works and Days] of Hesiod. Ancient Roman culture adapted the Greek myths to their own mythological traditions. Scholars have drawn more stories from the writings of Plutarch and Pausanias.

Archaeologists also have contributed to the body of contemporary knowledge about Greek myths, for many Greek artifacts portray scenes from the adventures. Heinrich Schliemann's discovery of the Mycenaean civilization as well as Sir Arthur Evans's discovery of the Minoan civilization unearthed sculptures, vases, and paintings that provided new details concerning the mythological characters and stories. Long after the ancient Greek and Roman civilizations crumbled, artists continued to find inspiration in Greek mythology. This influence waxed and waned, but most notably it resurfaced in the Italian Renaissance, when artists including Leonardo da Vinci, Michelangelo, and Raphael paired Greek mythology with Christian themes.

Academic interest in Greek mythology arose in Western culture at the end of the eighteenth century. Previously, Christian leaders tended to characterize the pagan stories as lies or fables, but by 1795, German scholar Johann Matthias Gesner argued for their historical value. Thereafter, in Germany and beyond, various interpretations arose concerning the myths. Some believed that the gods and heroes mentioned in the stories were once actual human beings, and that the myths had become exaggerated stories of their lives. Others immediately argued that the characters were allegorical, being symbols that represented characteristics or whole value systems, but not actual people. Still others argued that the myths arose from cultures in Asia and Asia minor, for some of the archaeological evidence suggested this trend. Though they could not agree on the details, early academics all believed the myths were valuable relics of an important period of history.

It was not until Edith Hamilton's *Mythology* that the stories became compiled in an understandable fashion for non-academics. Hamilton's anthology succeeds not only by telling these stories clearly to the modern reader but also by staying true, it seems, to the original cultures' narratives and voices. For decades, colleges and secondary schools around the world have assigned Hamilton's *Mythology* as a secure foundation for understanding the most important Greek myths. Thus, the book has captured the imaginations of academics and students alike.

Character List

Demeter

Goddess of the corn and harvest, Demeter is Persephone's mother, and she grieves every time her daughter goes down to Hades--these times correspond to earth's winter.

Persephone

Demeter's daughter, Persephone is kidnapped by Hades to become the wife of the underworld.

Hades

Hades is king of the underworld. He lives by the river Styx and kidnaps Persephone to become his queen.

Metaneira

Metaneira is a kind woman who takes in Demeter when the goddess comes down to earth in search of Persephone.

Dionysus

Son of Zeus and a mortal princess, Dionysus grows up in a verdant land and becomes god of wine.

Semele

Semele is a mortal woman with whom Zeus falls in love. She bears him Dionysus but dies when, at her wish, Zeus shows himself in all his glory.

Penthus

Penthus rules Thebes and dislikes Dionysus. In return, Dionysus arranges for women to tear him apart, limb by limb.

Gaea

Gaea is Mother of Earth. She marries Ouranos and gives birth to the first generation of earthly life: monsters and Titans.

Ouranos

Father Heaven marries Mother Earth and fathers the giants and Titans. A malicious god, Ouranos loses his power to his own son, Cronus.

Cronus

The son of Mother Earth and Father Heaven, Cronus is a Titan who rebels against his wicked father and takes power.

Rhea

Daughter of Mother Earth and Father Heaven, Rhea becomes her brother Cronus's queen when he takes power. Rhea swallows each of their children to prevent a prophecy that Cronus will be overthrown by his own son. She successfully sends away her sixth son, Zeus, but he fulfills the prophecy.

Zeus

Son of Rhea and Cronus, Zeus leads his siblings in a war against their father. When he wins, he becomes king of the gods.

Atlas

A Titan who loses in the war against Zeus and his siblings. His punishment is to hold the world on his shoulders for eternity.

Prometheus

Prometheus brings fire to humans and is punished greatly for doing so.

Epimetheus

Prometheus's brother, Epimetheus grants the animal kingdom so many gifts (fur, wings, shells, etc.) that there is about nothing left for man.

Pandora

Pandora opens a box she was supposed to leave closed. It releases all negative things into the world.

Io

Hera turns Io into a cow because Zeus is in love with her. Tied to his rock, Prometheus meets Io when she is a cow.

Hera

Hera is the wife of Zeus. She is a strong and wise goddess who is often jealous of her husband's interest in other humans.

Argus

Argus is a monster with one thousand eyes. Hera puts them in the peacock's tail.

Hermes

Son of Zeus and Hera, Hermes is the smartest god.

Cupid

The god of love, Cupid has magic arrows that make anyone fall in love with the next person he or she sees.

Europa

Europa is a mortal woman whom Zeus desires. Disguised as a bull, he carries her across an ocean to Crete, where she bears him two sons.

Polyphemus

Polyphemus is a Cyclops who traps Odysseus and his men in a cave. Polyphemus eats many of the men. He is immense and strong, but Odysseus proves more crafty and escapes.

Narcissus

Known for his beauty, Narcissus falls in love with his own reflection in a pond.

Echo

Echo is a beautiful nymph whom Zeus desires. Hera punishes her by deciding that she shall never speak first; she only shall repeat what others say.

Nemesis

God of anger, Nemesis punishes Narcissus by making the beautiful boy fall in love with his own reflection.

Hyacinthus

Apollo's best friend. Apollo accidentally kills him with a discus. The hyacinth flower grows on the ground where he died.

Adonis

A beautiful man, Adonis wins the affections of both Aphrodite and Persephone.

Psyche

A stunningly beautiful girl, Psyche wins the attention of Cupid but cannot resist seeing him in the light.

Venus

Goddess of love, Venus is also the mother of Cupid.

Pyramus

Pyramus falls in love with Thisbe, but when she arrives at their meeting spot, she sees a tiger and runs away. When she returns, she sees her lover, Thisbe, dead and then kills herself.

Thisbe

Thisbe falls in love with Pyramus. When he arrives at their meeting place, he finds her bloody shawl and kills himself. He does not realize that she dropped her shawl while running away from a tiger with blood in its mouth.

Orpheus

Orpheus is a talented musician who goes down to the underworld to save his lover, Eurydice. Unfortunately, he breaks his agreement and turns around to make sure she is following behind him on the way back up. She vanishes.

Eurydice

Eurydice is Orpheus's lover. She dies, goes down to the underworld, and almost returns to the living--but Orpheus fails to properly bring her back up.

Ceyx

Ceyx is happily married to Alcyone, but he decides to take a journey that ends with his drowning.

Alcyone

Alcyone, married to Ceyx, sees his body floating in the water. When she dives in after him, she turns into a bird.

Somnus

Somnus is the god of sleep, father of Morpheus.

Morpheus

Son of Somnus, Morpheus is known for telling Alcyone, in a dream, that her husband Ceyx has died.

Pygmalion

Pygmalion falls in love with his own art, a sculpture of a woman. Just when he accepts the hopelessness of the situation, Venus pities him and turns the sculpture into a woman.

Galetea

Venus turns Pygmalion's sculpture into a real woman, Galetea.

Baucis

Baucis, married to Philemon, welcomes Jupiter and Mercury into their home and thus is saved from a terrible flood.

Philemon

Married to Baucis, Philemon welcomes Jupiter and Mercury into their home and is thus saved from a terrible flood.

Endymion

Endymion is a beautiful man who, thanks to Selene, is in a magical slumber in which he sleeps forever.

Selene

Selene, a moon goddess, falls in love with Endymion and puts a magical spell on him so that he sleeps forever.

Daphne

A beautiful wood nymph, Daphne tries to outrun Apollo and turns into a laurel tree.

Alpheus

The river god who desires Arethusa.

Arethusa

A huntress who tries to run away from Alpheus, but Artemis turns her into a spring of water.

Phaethon

The son of Apollo, Phaethon asks his father to ride his chariot across the sky. He dies because the ride is too challenging.

Pegasus

Bellerophon's loyal, winged horse.

Glaucus

In the city of Corinth, Glaucus is an evil king who feeds his horses human flesh.

Bellerophon

Son of Poseidon, Bellerophon tames Pegasus with a golden bridle. After killing his brother by accident, Bellerophon takes Pegasus on many adventures in order to cleanse himself.

Proteus

After Bellerophon kills his brother by accident, he goes to King Proteus for purification. But when Proteus's wife makes advances on the young man, Proteus sends Bellerophon away to be killed.

Chimaera

The monster whom the Lycian king commands Bellerophon to kill.

Otus

Otus, twin to Ephialtes, considers himself better than the gods and eventually dies after he and his twin throw spears at each other.

Ephialtes

Ephialtes, twin to Otus, considers himself better than the gods and dies when he and his twin throw spears at each other.

Daedalus

A brilliant architect, Daedalus constructs the Labyrinth and escapes from it on a pair of home-made wings.

Icarus

Son of Daedalus, Icarus escapes from the Labyrinth on a pair of home-made wings. Unfortunately, he flies too high to the sun, the wings melt, and the boy plummets to his death.

King Acrisius

King Acrisius is told he will never have a son and that the son of his daughter will kill him. He tries to prevent the prophecy from coming true, but he cannot change fate, and his grandson Perseus kills him.

Danae

Daughter to King Acrisius, Danae lives in a bronze house because Acrisius does not want her to have the son who, according to prophecy, would kill him. Zeus, however, bears Danae a son named Perseus.

Dictys

A common fisherman, Dictys takes Danae and Perseus into his home when they wash up on on his island.

King Polydectes

Brother of Dictys, King Polydectes falls in love with Danae and asks Perseus to kill Medusa.

Perseus

One of the greatest heroes, Perseus is best known for killing Medusa. He also kills his father, King Acrisius.

The Gray Women

In order to get the correct sword to kill Medusa, Perseus goes to the Gray Women, three gray sisters with one eye to share among the three.

Andromeda

Perseus finds Andromeda chained to a rock and rescues her. She marries him.

Theseus

The great Athenian hero, Theseus is best known for killing the Minotaur with his bare hands.

Aegeus

King of Athens, Aegeus is father to Theseus. He jumps into the sea when his son returns from Crete sporting a black sail instead of a white one.

Minos

King Minos of Crete demands that every year, youths from Athens should come to Crete and be killed by the Minotaur in the Labyrinth. His daughter is Ariadne.

Ariadne

Daughter of King Minos, Ariadne helps Theseus find his way through the Labyrinth. She marries him but dies on the return to Athens.

Phaedra

Sister to Ariadne, Phaedra marries Theseus and falls madly in love with his son. She causes drama by claiming that he made advances on her, and she then kills herself.

Hippolytus

Son of Theseus, Hippolytus refuses advances from his step-mother, Phaedra. Believing him guilty, Theseus banishes him, and he dies at sea.

Minotaur

A half bull, half human, the Minotaur lives inside the Labyrinth and kills innocent Athenian youth until Theseus kills him.

Hercules

One of the greatest Greek heroes, Hercules is known for his unmatched strength and amazing achievements.

Princess Megara

Married to Hercules, Megara bears him three sons. Hercules kills his sons after Hera sends him insanity.

Eurystheus

Eurystheus sends Hercules on many journeys so that Hercules can cleanse himself from the guilt of having killed his own sons.

Cerebrus

The three-headed dog who lives in Hades.

Atalanta

Raised by a she-bear, Atalanta is faster than all her suitors. She races them and is winning, but she loses because she is distracted by golden apples.

Melanion/Hippomenes

Known as both Melanion and Hippomenes, this crafty character beats Atalanta in a race by dropping golden apples along the way.

Nephele

The wife of Athamas. Once he gets sick of her, she lands in jail.

Athamas

A Greek king, Athamas jails his wife Nephele when he becomes sick of her. He marries a young princess, who convinces him to offer his son, Phrixus, as a sacrifice to the gods.

Phrixus

Son of Athamas and Nephele, Phrixus almost dies as a sacrifice to the gods, but instead a ram with a golden fleece saves him and his sister.

King Etes

Saved by the ram with golden fleece, Phrixus arrives at the country of Colchis and gives the fleece to King Etes.

King Pelias

Pelias steals the crown from his brother and sends his nephew, Jason, on many adventures. Eventually, his own daughter kills him.

Jason

Jason overcomes many obstacles, most notably winning the golden fleece, in order to win back the crown from his wicked uncle Pelias. He marries Medea but later marries another woman.

Medea

Medea helps Jason get the golden fleece and marries him. But when he later marries someone else, she kills the new wife as well as the two sons she bore to Jason.

Tantalus

Son of Zeus, Tantalus murders his own son, Pelops, and tries to feed him to the gods without their knowing. The gods punish him by "tantalizing" him with food and water for eternity.

Pelops

Tantalus's son, murdered by his father and served to the gods as food. The gods bring him back to life, and he eventually has a daughter, Niobe.

Niobe

Daughter to Pelops, Niobe believes herself to be better than the gods, specifically the goddess Leto. Artemis and Apollo, therefore, shoot deadly arrows into all fourteen of Niobe's children. Niobe becomes a stone, always covered in tears.

Iphigenia

Sister of Orestes, Iphigenia almost dies as a human sacrifice, but she is saved by Athena. She is finally reunited with her brother and lives happily.

Orestes

Orestes, brother to Iphigenia, comes to her island and almost dies at her hand. Thanks to Athena, he lives with her happily.

Pylades

Orestes's friend, who travels with him to Iphigenia's island.

King Laius

Father of Oedipus, King Laius tries and fails to change the prophecy that his own son will kill him.

Oedipus

Son of King Laius and Jocasta, Oedipus unknowingly kills his father and marries his mother.

Jocasta

Oedipus's mother, Jocasta unknowingly marries her son. Horrified when this truth is revealed, she kills herself.

Antigone

Son of Oedipus and Jocasta, Antigone is known for her loyalty to her brother, Polyneices, whom she buries against the king's law. She dies for this noble act.

Ismene

Daughter of Oedipus and Jocasta.

Polyneices

Son of Oedipus and Jocasta, Polyneices dies by fighting the illegitimate king, Creon. His sister, Antigone, buries him against Creon's order.

Eteocles

One of Jocasta's and Oedipus's four children. He and his brother, Polyneices, kill each other.

Creon

Jocasta's brother, Creon becomes king after Oedipus exiles himself to an island and Jocasta dies. He kills Antigone for burying her brother.

Major Themes

Heroism

Greek heroes tend to share uncommon strength, immense bravery, and noble morality. They also depend upon a certain degree of clever ingenuity to achieve success. For example, Perseus could not have killed Medusa if he did not have the smarts to steal the Gray Women's eye. Exceeding the limits of average men, the heroes act somewhere between gods and mortals in the hierarchy of the Greek myths. Their stories are some of the most memorable; consider Theseus, Hercules, and Perseus. Through these figures, the modern reader can understand many Greek values.

Generosity

Throughout the Greek myths, generosity appears to be noble. Sometimes, generosity subtly reinforces a story, such as when Metaneira takes in Demeter, disguised as an elderly woman, or when Dictys takes in baby Perseus and Danae when they wash up on his shore. Hospitality is a particularly important species of generosity. In the case of Baucis and Philemon, the theme is much more pronounced. When the poor couple take two travelers into their home, they have no idea that Jupiter and Mercury are testing their hospitality. Their selfless behavior saves them from the flood and secures their respect in the eyes of the gods. In these generosity stories, one can see a way in which Greek myths were used as morality tales, explaining what is right and what is wrong, how to live and how not to live. Generosity, altruism, or freely giving to others may not seem to be in the immediate interest of the giver, which might be why these myths reinforce the idea that it is a good quality that should be valued.

Faith

Faith is perhaps the most widely important theme in Greek mythology. For one thing, those who hear the myths must in some way believe they are true in order for them to be meaningful. Humans, not only those in the myths but also those who hear the myths, generally go even further and believe that the gods actually exist. Characters who defy or anger the gods are punished, and those who honor and praise the gods find rewards. Having faith in a prophecy is better than trying to circumvent it. Faith also appears in more nuanced situations having to do with trust and belief. Psyche, for example, cannot bear to not see her husband during the daylight, so she chooses to see Cupid in the light, against his wishes. Although eventually she redeems herself from this betrayal, it takes much suffering and effort. Orpheus, by contrast, finds no forgiveness when he loses his faith while leading Eurydice up from the underworld. Such myths reinforce the theme that faith should not be broken or misused.

Love

Love appears throughout the Greek myths and often drives the narrative forward. However, different kinds of love emerge in the text with different implications. In some instances, love is visceral and impulsive, caused by Cupid's arrow. This kind of love causes Alpheus to chase Arethusa, Apollo to chase Daphne, or Zeus to take Europa across an ocean on his back. Such love is characterized by intense feeling and frenzy. Alternatively, we see in the Greek myths a less exciting but ultimately longer lasting kind of love. Ceyx and Alcyone become birds who fly together for eternity after they die. Mulberry grows from the blood of Pyramus and Thisbe. And Baucis and Philemon become intertwined trees when they die. In these instances, love exists among mortals in an eternal realm, and it is perhaps the closest that most humans can ever approach godliness in the myths.

Fate

Throughout the myths, fate appears as a powerful force that no human or god may contend with. Cronus received a prophecy that he would be overthrown by his son, as did King Laius. Both men tried to prevent the outcome, and both failed. In this sense, mankind and gods share a similarly naive character when it comes to reconciling themselves to fate. But these tales raise the question of who controls fate, if not the gods. Is there an even higher power than those on Mount Olympus, if even the gods cannot control fate? Or is fate just a way of characterizing the truth about what will happen at a future time?

Strange Love

In several instances, variations of strange love present complex challenges in Greek mythology. Narcissus, for example, falls in love with his own image and cannot leave it alone for one moment. He withers and dies by the pool in which he sees his own reflection. Selene falls in love with Endymion and hopes to keep him forever by making him sleep forever. Unfortunately, she suffers from loneliness. In both of these circumstances, a selfish kind of love results in suffering. In the case of Pygmalion, Venus rewards his love for his sculpture, but only when he himself decides that it is not healthy for him to give such affection to an inanimate object. As if rewarding his realistic maturity, Venus then turns the piece of stone into a real woman. Perhaps the unifying theme of these examples of strange love is that true love is mutually felt from both parties but that such love is very difficult when it involves two natures, such as human and beast, human and sculpture, or divinity and human.

Sacrifice

Sacrifices recur throughout the Greek myths, not just because physical sacrifice was significant in ancient Greek societies. Antigone stands as the best example, for she sacrifices herself in order to bury her brother. Pyramus and Thisbe sacrifice themselves for each other. Baucis and Philemon sacrifice their comfort in order to house two travelers in their small house. In these and other cases, heroism becomes something not just reserved for strong people (like Hercules) but a quality that any common person can achieve. Through sacrifice, characters are rewarded by gods and stand as good examples to the characters surrounding them. In the case of Baucis and Philemon, this example is so extreme that the gods flood out everyone else in the village. While it is not easy, as Prometheus can attest, sacrifice often must be made for the sake of honor and morality rather than simply out of the love of one's own.

Glossary of Terms

Ambrosia

The food or drink of the gods.

Discus

A heavy disc thrown in competition.

Hyacinth

A plant with perhaps blood-colored flowers, commemorating the death of Hyacinthus by Apollo.

Laurel tree

The bay tree, an evergreen with a pleasant scent.

Mount Olympus

The mountain upon which the Greek gods reside.

Mulberry

A tree that produces a sweet berry.

Nymph

A female, human-like spirit bound to a particular place in nature.

Oracle

A giver of wisdom and prophecy. The Oracle of Delphi often gave ambiguous responses to questions, leaving the interpretation up to others.

Pomegranate

Considered the "food of the dead," a temptingly sweet and attractive fruit with tiny seeds, which also suggests fertility.

Prophecy

A prediction of what is to come.

Theban

A person from Thebes, a city about halfway from Athens to Delphi and at one time a serious rival to Athens.

Short Summary

The stories of mythology involve many tales about the gods and their interactions with each other and with mortals. The stories begin at the beginning of time and proceed through the first few generations of gods and goddesses until they begin to interact with humans. Doing so creates a wide variety of troubles for humans and gods alike.

Persephone: When Persephone is captured by Hades, her mother Demeter refuses to let the crops grow on earth. Zeus demands Persephone's return, but because she ate the pomegranate seed, she must return to the Underworld for several months each year.

Dionysus: Dionysus grew up in a verdant land and became the wine god. Like wine itself, he proves himself to be alternatively fun and harsh.

The Creation of the Earth: From the beginning of time, gods have fought over who controls the earth. Finally, Zeus wins the war and takes charge.

Prometheus: Prometheus grants humans the gift of fire, and Zeus becomes extremely angry. As punishment, Zeus ties Prometheus to a rock.

Pandora: As more punishment against the gift Prometheus gave humans, Zeus put all misfortunes into a box that the curious Pandora then opens.

Prometheus and Io: In the form of a cow, Io finds Prometheus tied to his rock. As the two characters empathize with one another, Prometheus tells Io her fortune and gives her courage to keep living.

Europa: Zeus pursues a fine maiden, Europa, in the shape of a bull. He takes her on a ride across the ocean and eventually bears two sons by her.

The Cyclops Polyphemus: The evil Cyclops traps Odysseus and his men inside a cave until Odysseus blinds the monster and escapes under the bellies of Polyphemus's rams.

Narcissus: A beautiful boy falls in love with his own reflection in a river. Eventually he perishes there.

Echo: A nymph named Echo falls in love with Narcissus, but Hera places a spell on her that allows her only to repeat spoken words but never to speak first.

Hyacinthus: Apollo and Hyacinthus are best friends, but Apollo accidentally kills Hyacinthus as they compete in a discus-throwing contest. Flowers grow where Hyacinthus dies.

Adonis: Adonis is a beautiful young man who wins the attentions of both Persephone and Aphrodite. Eventually he is killed by a wild boar.

Cupid and Psyche: Venus is jealous of a beautiful girl named Psyche, who wins the attention of her son Cupid. Although Psyche marries Cupid, she disobeys him and demands to see his figure in the light. Disowned by her husband, she then sets out to win his love and respect, and after many adventures, she eventually does.

Pyramus and Thisbe: Two young lovers run away to be with each other but accidentally lead each other to their deaths.

Orpheus and Eurydice: Eurydice dies when a viper stings her, and her lover, Orpheus, goes down to the Underworld to bring her back. Hades agrees, but when Orpheus fails to abide by his one condition (that he not turn around as he leads Eurydice back up), his lover goes back down to the Underworld.

Ceyx and Alcyone: Ceyx leaves his lover, Alcyone, and dies at sea. Alcyone jumps into the ocean for his body, and the two lovers turn into birds.

Daphne: Apollo chases after Daphne, who refuses his advances. Just before he catches her, she turns into a laurel tree.

Pygmalion: A talented artist falls in love with a sculpture he made of a woman. Just when he gives up on the futile relationship, Venus takes pity and turns the statue into a living woman.

Baucis and Philemon: When Jupiter and Mercury come down to earth to test humans' hospitality, only one elderly couple, Baucis and Philemon, prove generous. The gods reward the couple and grant them their wish of becoming intertwining trees when they die.

Endymion: A beautiful boy, Endymion, wins the affection of the Moon Goddess, Selene. She puts him under a spell that makes him forever asleep and continues to be lonely.

Arethusa and Alpheus: Arethusa, a mortal huntress, wins the attention of the river god, Alpheus. Arethusa wants nothing to do with him, so to spare her from rape, Artemis turns her into a river spring.

Phaethon: A young man, Phaethon, discovers that Apollo is his father and asks to ride the god's chariot. He does so against all advice and gets completely out of control until Zeus strikes him down with a thunderbolt.

Bellerophon: Bellerophon accidentally kills his brother. To purify himself, he rides Pegasus as he completes challenges.

Otus and Ephialtes: Otus and Ephialtes are two rambunctious and enormous twins, the sons of Poseidon, who believe themselves to be better than gods. Finally, Artemis takes revenge against their actions by tricking them into killing each other.

Daedalus: Deadalus, the brilliant architect who designed the labyrinth, devises wings to help him and his son, Icarus, escape King Minos. Against his father's warning, however, Icarus flies too close to the sun. His wings melt, and he falls to his death.

Perseus: One of the great Greek heroes, Perseus kills the Medusa and overcomes seemingly impossible challenges.

Theseus: A great Athenian hero, Theseus defeats the Minotaur with the help of Ariadne, whom he later marries.

Hercules: Considered the greatest Greek hero (and certainly the strongest), Hercules kills his children when Hera puts him under a spell. To purify himself, he embarks on incredible challenges and succeeds.

The Quest for the Golden Fleece: When Jason claims his rightful place as king, the reigning king, Pelias, demands that he acquire the golden fleece. With the help of Medea, Jason gets the fleece.

Tantalus: Tantalus loses favor with the gods after he murders all his children. As punishment, they "tantalize" him by putting food and water in front of him but never allowing him to eat or drink.

Iphigenia: Iphigenia is saved from human sacrifice and made queen of an island. She almost kills her own brother, Orestes, but with the help of the gods, they escape together.

Antigone: Antigone buries her brother despite the king's imposition of a law to the contrary. She is killed for the act but achieves honor in the process.

Oedipus: Unknowingly, Oedipus fulfills a prophecy by killing his father and marrying his mother. Tragedy unfolds as he learns the awful truth.

Summary and Analysis of Persephone; Dionysus (Bacchus)

Demeter, goddess of the corn and harvest, has one daughter, Persephone, the maiden of spring. Hades, god of the Underworld, kidnaps Persephone and brings her down to be his wife in the Underworld. Grief-stricken and confused, Demeter withholds her gifts from the world, which becomes "a frozen desert." She comes down to human beings in the form of an elderly woman and is taken in by a woman named Metaneira. At night, Demeter attempts to grant Metaneira's son immortal youth by secretly anointing the boy with ambrosia and placing him in a hot fire. When Metaneira discovers Demeter putting her son in the fire, she becomes irate. Demeter then sheds her disguise and demands that the people of the town build her a temple.

In this temple, far removed from the other gods in Olympus, Demeter sits in longing for her daughter. The earth, meanwhile, freezes to a bitter cold that threatens mankind's extinction. Finally, Zeus intervenes by telling Hermes to go down to the underworld and bring Persephone back. Hades knows he must agree to Zeus's terms, but he gives Persephone a pomegranate seed, knowing that if she eats it she will have to return to him. With her daughter back, Demeter leaves her temple and joins the other gods on Mount Olympus. But because Persephone does eat the pomegranate seed, she must return to the Underworld for four months a year. In these months, Demeter grieves and the earth goes through winter.

...

Dionysus, son of Zeus and a mortal Theban princess, is the only god whose parents were not both divine. Zeus was madly in love with a mortal, Semele, and he promised her that he would do anything for her. She asked to see him in all his glory as the King of Heaven, and although Zeus knew that it would kill her to see him this way, he held to his word. As Semele died, Zeus took her almost-born child and brought him to be raised by nymphs in a particularly lush, verdant land. Dionysus, the wine-god, thus grows up among rain and foliage, and by the time he is an adult he has rescued his mother from the Underworld and brought her to Olympus, where she has been allowed to reside because she gave birth to a god.

Dionysus, meanwhile, builds a following of mortals known for wearing ivy leaves, running through the forest, and drinking wine. These followers, mostly women, travel with Dionysus to Thebes, the city where Semele lived when she was alive. Penthus, who rules Thebes, becomes quite disturbed by the loud, wine-drinking women and by Dionysus himself. He insults Dionysus, jails him, and refuses to believe that he is dealing with a deity. Dionysus responds by sending Penthus to the hills to meet his clan of female followers. Then, Dionysus shows his cruel power: he makes his followers mad. All the women mistake Penthus for a mountain beast and rush to destroy him. They tear him apart, limb by limb, and Penthus finally understands that he has insulted a god and must pay for that mistake with his life.

Once Penthus has been sufficiently torn apart, Dionysus returns his followers to their senses.

Analysis

Like many myths, the story of Persephone does more than account for a natural phenomenon such as the seasons. This story shows the emotional complexity of Demeter; she is a god who suffers. Persephone too suffers, for every year she must return to the Underworld. These two figures provide touchstones for people who are grappling with death or grief. As for Metaneira, her hospitality is undercut by her anger at Demeter's generous response.

The story of Persephone also reveals a trend in Greek mythology in which different gods represent different aspects of the natural world. Persephone comes to represent spring, and Demeter represents summer. Zeus, often associated with lightning bolts, remains most powerfully positioned in the sky. By defining characters through natural elements, the Greek myths succeed in making the characters and morals relevant to the everyday person's life.

Many scholars note that the story of Persephone captures the important spirit of the natural process. As the descent and return of the goddess bring about the seasons, so too does her transition resemble the birth-and-death cycle of all living things. One of the most innocent characters in Greek mythology, Persephone shows that youth must eventually grow old and die.

Finally, the story of Persephone revolves around a crucial symbol: the pomegranate seed. Considered the "food of the dead," the fruit suggests the deceptive nature of the Underworld, for although the pomegranate is temptingly sweet and attractive, its power is strong and irreversible.

The story of Dionysus shows the binary nature of this god. Like wine itself, Dionysus can cause extreme joy but also drunken confusion. This dual nature of being man's benefactor and man's destroyer is not just a moral reminder about the effects of wine. It expresses a common dichotomy in the myth literature, reflecting the Greek interest in balance. Throughout the mythology, the ideal of balance emerges after characters tend to find trouble when they seek extremes. Gods often punish extreme behavior and reward a balanced, grateful, and graceful way of living.

Dionysus's tale reveals a way in which Greek myths served to enforce a moral code. Although some tales are more complex than others, they tend to hold moral significance for the reader. In this case, the story of Dionysus reminds the reader that bad deeds will be remembered and revenge will ensue.

The Dionysus story is also important because it is one of the few instances in which a character goes into the Underworld and out again. In this case, it takes a god to retrieve the human. Dionysus rescues his mother and experiences a kind of life after death, thus also representing resurrection. A similar feeling might come to pass among someone who has just become sober.

Summary and Analysis of Persephone; Dionysus (Bacchus)

Summary and Analysis of The Creation of the Earth

Mother Earth (Gaea) and Father Heaven (Ouranos) give birth to the first generations of life on earth. Some of their children are monsters, with power as great as volcanoes, but without a distinct character like individual humans. Three of these monsters have one hundred hands and fifty heads. Three others have only one eye in the middle of their foreheads and are known as the Cyclopses. Besides the monsters, Earth and Heaven give birth to a race of Titans, who are large, powerful, and not necessarily malevolent. Father Heaven is malicious and mean, however, treating his children horribly, even locking up all his monster children in a cave in the earth. Distraught by this behavior, Mother Earth begs her children to rebel against him. Only one does, a Titan named Cronus (Saturn).

From then on, Cronus becomes ruler of the universe with his sister, Rhea, as queen. It was prophesized that Cronus would be overthrown by his own son, so every time they have a child, Cronus swallows him or her. But Rhea succeeds in sending her sixth child secretly to Crete. In order to do so, Rhea wraps a rock in swaddling clothes, which the king swallows instead of the child.

Eventually when the son, Zeus, grows up, he rebels against Cronus and forces him to disgorge his five brothers and sisters. A war breaks out with the Titans, led by Cronus, against Zeus and his siblings. Zeus wins the war partially because he releases all the monsters from the cave in the earth, and also because one Titan, Prometheus, sides with him.

When he rises to power, Zeus punishes all the Titans and monsters who fought against him. He punishes a Titan named Atlas (brother of Prometheus) by forcing him "to bear on his back forever the cruel strength of the crushing world." Although two small rebellions attempt to remove Zeus and his siblings from power, the gods establish themselves as the new rulers of the universe.

Analysis

This creation story sets a foundation for the Greek myths. With this history established, Zeus and his siblings are clearly the ruling powers on Mount Olympus. Zeus has won a kind of divine order for the universe in which he metes out justice. In the generations of the Titans and of Ouranos, there was a fair amount of chaos and monstrosity. By the time of Zeus, however, the divinities seem a bit more human. We will meet the gods who are more like Zeus time and time again.

Fate is stronger even than Cronus, a second-generation divinity. In this way, the myth raises a fundamental question: who controls fate? Are his parents still somehow in charge? Although many stories seem to suggest that the gods control the fate of all things, this tale reveals that some powers may be beyond everyone's control. By leaving such fundamental questions unanswered, the myth refuses to make it easy for the reader to develop a concept of fate; it is mysterious. In the future, fate will continue to be unstoppable, despite everyone's best efforts to circumvent it, and it will be no less mysterious when all the attempts to circumvent fate actually contribute to its inevitable unfolding.

The creation story also sets a basis for seeing the world as one of conflict rather than cooperation. With such fighting and violence in its very foundation, it is no wonder that harsh punishments and tough realities are to come. Indeed, the myths often present a dog-eat-dog world in which kindness is rare and forgiveness even rarer, one where strength in battle is often the key to success. This is not to downplay the value of love and friendship in other myths, but it is perhaps to show why such relationships are of special value in such a conflicted world.

Note that the first generation of divinities includes something of a gender balance: there are both a mother and a father. By the time of Zeus, a single male god is in control. If the gods are to be examples for humans, good or bad, which generation should be the model for human rule? Zeus's regime, that of a single male king, is the one that succeeds.

Summary and Analysis of Prometheus; Pandora; Prometheus and Io

Zeus gives the task of creating humans to Prometheus and his brother Epimetheus. Epimetheus, whose name means "afterthought," grants the animal kingdom all the joys of creation—fur, wings, shells, and so on—until there seems to be nothing left for man. He appeals to Prometheus for help.

Prometheus takes over and devises a way to make mankind superior to the animals. First, he gives mankind an upright shape like that of the gods. Then, he travels to the sun, where he lights a torch and brings fire down to the earth. Zeus resents the great advantages that Prometheus has given man, but he cannot undo the gifts. He punishes Prometheus by binding him to a rock and condemning him to a life of "no rest, no sleep, no moment's respite."

Zeus once received a prophecy that a son of his would one day overthrow him—and that only Prometheus would know that son's name. Despite threats, Prometheus does not cave in to Zeus's pressure, instead choosing to endure an eagle's feasting on his flesh and liver every day.

...

As further revenge against Prometheus and the powers he has given man, Zeus creates a woman named Pandora. Zeus gives her a box and forbids her from opening it. He sends her down to earth, where her insatiable curiosity leads her to open the lid. Out fly plagues, sorrow, mischief, and all other misfortunes that can plague mankind. Horrified, Pandora attempts to shut the lid of the box, but it is too late. The only good element to fly out of the box is hope.

...

Prometheus, tied to his rock, sees a strange visitor: a cow that speaks like a girl. Her voice is laden with pain and sorrow, but it sounds beautiful. This is Io, and she tells Prometheus her story. She used to be a beautiful young woman, and Zeus fell in love with her. When Zeus's jealous wife Hera suspected their relationship, Zeus turned Io into a heifer. The shrewd Hera asked for the heifer as a present, and Zeus reluctantly gave Io away. Hera put Io in the care of Argus, a monster with one thousand eyes, so that Zeus could never get her back.

Zeus missed Io terribly and regretted her unfortunate transformation, so he pleaded with his son Hermes, the messenger god, to find a way of killing Argus. Hermes, known as the smartest god, disguised himself as a country fellow and approached Argus. The thousand-eyed monster invited Hermes to sit next to him, and Hermes started playing on a pipe of reeds as sweetly and monotonously as possible. Eventually Argus fell asleep, Hermes killed him, and Hera put the thousand eyes in the feathers of her favorite bird, the peacock. It seemed that Io would be free, but Hera sent a fly to follow her and drive her insane.

In response to the story, Prometheus reveals a prophecy that Io will wander for a long time in the beastly body, tormented by the fly. But finally she will reach the river Nile, where Zeus will restore her to her human form and give her a son. From this son will be born the greatest of heroes, Hercules, who will give Prometheus himself his freedom.

Analysis

Prometheus is most notable for his heroic strength. Although Zeus severely punishes the very Titan who helped him come to power, Prometheus never yields to the god's threats. Hamilton notes that despite slight variations on the Prometheus tale, his reputation remains intact; he is a "rebel against injustice and the authority of power."

In this way, the myths present an important aspect of the Greek conception of a hero: the ability to suffer immense challenges. As we meet other heroes in later tales, other aspects of a hero's character will come out. With Prometheus, the story emphasizes his quiet resolve and incredible strength. This humanizes the hero, making him humble and decent, as any reader of the myth might want to be.

Mankind enjoys few or none of the external benefits enjoyed by animals, such as fur coats or protective shells. Instead, humans have been given fire, representing human power over energy. Human ingenuity is necessary to convert fire and energy to human purposes. Fire is a heavenly gift, having come from the sun and from a god.

In the famous story of Pandora's box, the reader learns how earthly hardship was born. It is interesting to note that the female (and her curiosity) is blamed for all human suffering, like Eve in the Judeo-Christian tradition. Scholars have pointed to this fact in association with the Adam and Eve story, in which Eve is said to have ruined the utopia where mankind once lived. Retribution, a recurring theme in mythology, is quite notable in the story of Pandora. The Greek gods tend to lash out harshly when they perceive wrong done to them, and the case of Pandora is no exception. She was sent to earth so that her curiosity would drive her to open the box.

The Pandora story also underscores Zeus's crafty nature. From Pandora's box, mortals and gods alike understand the power of the god and fear his authority—at the same time, by leaving the fault in Pandora's lap, he avoids direct responsibility for the evils in the world.

Interestingly, hope came out of the box, too. Does that mean that hope could be a misfortune as well? Perhaps, if hope represents a clinging to that which is untrue and does not exist. Or perhaps, if hope is not a misfortune, hope represents the kindness in Zeus's heart, in that he grants mankind the ability to aspire and improve despite the evils released from the box.

The myth of Prometheus and Io shows how the enduring spirit of Prometheus is refigured in the suffering Io. As the two suffering beings meet on the craggy rock, they share a common injustice and pain. By telling the prophecy to Io, Prometheus gives her hope that will help her stay strong in the hard times ahead.

As the two characters connect, the story portrays a poignant scene of empathy between characters who do not resemble on another: one character in a human form and the other in the form of a cow. Although characters take different forms throughout Greek mythology, rarely do we see such strong connections between characters of different physical shapes. In this subtle way, the myth suggests that character and spirit are separate from the physical body. Does one's nature change if one's appearance changes?

The story that Io tells Prometheus also reveals much about the relationship between Zeus and Hera. They trick each other, they play games with each other, and they use humans as pawns in those games. In his retelling of these events, the writer Ovid remarks that lies told by lovers are not wrong, but neither are they very useful: Hera knew exactly what Zeus was up to all along. In this sense, she is a counter-example versus many of the weak, naive, or innocent female characters throughout mythology. Shrewd and proactive, Hera outwits her husband as much as she can.

It is interesting to note that the story of Prometheus and Io also introduces the greatest of all heroes, Hercules. We learn about him in later myths, some of the most famous of the Greek canon.

Summary and Analysis of Prometheus; Pandora; Prometheus and...

Summary and Analysis of Europa; the Cyclops Polyphemus

Cupid hits Zeus with an arrow, and the god instantly falls in love with a pretty mortal maiden, Europa. That morning, Europa awakens from a strange dream in which two different continents were fighting over her. She goes down to the ocean with her friends to bathe and pick flowers, and Zeus arrives disguised as a magnificent bull. Europa climbs on top of his back, and as soon as she does, Zeus gallops away. Europa clings tightly to his horn as they gallop over the ocean. Terrified, she understands that this must be a god, and she begs Zeus to let her go. But Zeus comforts Europa, explaining that he loves her and will bring her to his home island, Crete. When they arrive, Zeus transforms himself into a human and makes love to her. The people of Crete greet Europa with a bridal ceremony. She settles on the island and eventually bears Zeus two sons.

...

At the creation of the world, there were only three Cyclops, but they reproduced and had many offspring. They crafted Zeus's thunderbolts and were known for their strength and hostility to strangers. Thus, when Odysseus (Ulysses) sails for home from Troy and beaches his boat on their shore, great dangers await. Odysseus and his crew see a cave on the beach and walk inside to explore. The enormous Polyphemus pushes a huge rock over the cave's opening, effectively trapping the men inside. He eats a few men and falls asleep. The situation seems hopeless, but Odysseus comes up with a plan. He finds an enormous timber and sharpens the end of it. Odysseus then offers Polyphemus his wine, which the beast drinks. The Cyclops promptly falls asleep. As the Cyclops sleeps, Odysseus and his men heat the tip of the sharpened log in a fire and then ram it into Polyphemus's eye, blinding him. Polyphemus is still determined to kill all the men, but they escape from the cave under the bellies of Polyphemus's rams, which are out at pasture.

Analysis

Like the story of Io, the story of Europa depicts Zeus in desperate desire of a mortal maiden. But unlike Io, Europa never suffers much. Hamilton notes that it is unclear why Hera never opposes this relationship. Is she just preoccupied? Does the fact that Cupid was the agent mean that Zeus is not responsible? Or perhaps, since Hera is a strong and crafty woman, she was preoccupied with some mischief of her own. The myth leaves this issue for the reader to interpret.

This story also provides a good example of a human who trusts the gods. Although she is frightened to ride on a bull across the ocean, Europa trusts Zeus when he says he loves her and will not do her harm. Note that this is one of many myths in which a god appears to a human in animal or human form. In such cases it is clear that the divine nature is not lost, though the god picks up, for a time, some of the qualities of the animal.

Also, note that Zeus is identified here with a particular place on earth, the island of Crete. The gods are not really everywhere at all times as in some religious traditions; they tend to be in one place or another like mortal beings are, even though they also can act at a distance when necessary.

The theme of reciprocity arises throughout Greek mythology, and in Europa's trusting nature, it is evident. Only good things come to her when she trusts Zeus: she bears children and lives a happy life on Crete. The question then arises whether it is better to give in to the gods against one's wishes or to suffer the consequences of fighting for what one wants. The question is complicated because of the varying kinds of punishments that are meted out against the unfaithful, sometimes very severe.

The tale of Odysseus and the Cyclops is one of the most classic stories of the Greek tradition. It is told in Homer's Odyssey, which details Odysseus's various adventures while journeying home from war. This story shows the heroism and craftiness of Odysseus. Although Odysseus also is very strong, the story demonstrates the advantage of clever thinking in addition to brute strength.

The story of Polyphemus also reveals important aspects of Greek heroism: leadership and courage under pressure. None of Odysseus's men has the sense to plot an escape from the cave; only their leader creates the plan and engages in the main execution of the plan. While some traits of Greek heroes serve to humble the heroic characters and bring them down to an accessible level, in this case Odysseus shows that he is truly greater than the average man.

Polyphemus himself provides an interesting example of a villainous monster. Although demons pepper the myths, Polyphemus stands out as particularly memorable for his vicious, man-eating behavior. Ugly, enormous, and terrifying, he symbolizes all the difficult challenges that threaten mankind. Importantly, Odysseus uses his mind to overcome these challenges, and thus the myth suggests that human ingenuity is our greatest asset in the face of danger.

Summary and Analysis of Narcissus; Hyacinth; Adonis

Narcissus is the most beautiful boy whom many have ever seen, but he does not return anyone's affections. One of the disappointed nymphs prays to the god of anger, Nemesis, that "he who loves not others love himself." Nemesis answers this prayer. Narcissus looks at his own reflection in a river and suddenly falls in love with himself. He can think of nothing and no one else. He pines away, leaning perpetually over the pool, until finally he perishes.

The story of Narcissus includes the story of Echo, a nymph who falls in love with him. Echo falls under an unfortunate spell cast by Hera, who has suspected that Zeus is interested in her or, at least, in one of her nymph friends. Hera determines that Echo will always have the last word but never have the power to speak first. That is, she only can repeat other people's utterances. When the dying Narcissus calls "farewell" to his own image, Echo can only repeat the words—a final good-bye. In the place where Narcissus dies, a beautiful flower grows, and the nymphs call it Narcissus.

...

Apollo and Hyacinthus are best friends. They compete to see who can throw a discus the farthest. In the competition, Apollo accidentally throws his discus into Hyacinthus, killing him. As Apollo holds the body of his best friend, he wishes that he himself would stop living so that the beautiful, young Hyacinthus could live on. As he speaks those words, the blood spilling from the dying youth turns the grass green, and a beautiful flower grows—the hyacinth.

...

Adonis is an extremely handsome young man, and Aphrodite falls in love with him. She puts him in Persephone's care, but she also falls in love with him. Finally, Zeus intervenes and decides that Adonis shall spend half the year with Persephone and half the year with Aphrodite. One day, Adonis hunts a wild boar and thinks he killed it. But the boar was only wounded, and it fiercely lunges at Adonis as he approaches. Aphrodite flies to him and holds him, dying, in her arms. Flowers grow where the blood wets the ground.

Analysis

The story of Narcissus concerns the dangers of self-love. Western culture often returns to consider the nature of the self-absorbed individual. Literature, art, and philosophy have investigated the relative importance of self-love. Here, the extreme form of self-love is figured as a warning.

Echo is yet another unfortunate female who is a victim of Hera's jealousy. The sad story of Echo's unrequited love and Narcissus's perverted love reveals the importance of natural imagery in Greek myths. Echo reflects the echoes people hear across empty spaces, and wildflowers were revered as physical reminders of a Greek's beauty and fertility.

Together, the stories of Narcissus and Echo represent the tragedy of missed connections, for they both love wrongly. Narcissus loves simply a reflection; Echo loves someone who cannot love another. The Greek myths thus explore sad scenarios that leave certain characters unhappy or unfulfilled. It seems that the gods have the power to make everything "right" and could make love reciprocal, but they rarely choose to do so. From the troubles of love arise many the complex dramas of the human condition.

In the story of Narcissus, natural imagery stands out. Typical of Greek mythology, elements in nature take on narrative significance and add a particular attitude to a tale. By setting the stories in such idyllic, natural settings as by the river where Narcissus falls in love with himself, the Greek storytellers conjured an imaginary world in which beauty and nature rule the imagination.

The short myth of Apollo and Hyacinthus concerns the fragility of living. It seems strange that such an impressive god as Apollo should make such a tragic mistake, but this story shows a rare instance in which a god regrets an action and a time in which fate goes against a god's wishes. The tragedy of error thus extends to the powerful gods, not just the mortals on earth.

The story also warns against the dangers of competition, for it is in this context that Hyacinthus dies. Competitions arise throughout Greek mythology, and not always to tragic effect. But in almost every case, competitions cause an important or dramatic situation to occur.

Perhaps most importantly, the story of Hyacinthus concerns the cyclical relationship between life and death. Just after Hyacinthus dies, he is in a sense reborn as a flower. As in other stories of life after death, Hyacinthus's new form as a flower suggests that life cycles can recur from one natural state to another. In this case, it is hard to see what Hyacinthus retains of his human nature in having become a flower.

Finally, the story displays an unusually human portrayal of a god. As good friends do, the two men share love and loyalty; Apollo shows both masculine heroism and sensitive compassion. Indeed, his love for his friend appears to be the main reason why Hyacinthus is able to live on.

Another tragic love story is that of Adonis, though in this case, Adonis is killed by his own error and by an animal. The key mistake is thinking that the boar is dead when it is alive. This myth also indicates more about mortality. Aphrodite can do nothing to bring the mortal back to life; she cannot even go into the underworld and bring him back. The flowers that grow in Adonis's place suggest hope and life after death, just as they do with Hyacinthus.

Adonis's story also reveals the competitive nature of the gods, for both Persephone and Aphrodite fight for his attention until finally Zeus resolves the fight. In this sense, they act like immature humans, unable to reach common ground without the help of an authority. Alternatively, the bickering between Persephone and Aphrodite may reveal that human concerns are indeed so significant and critical that they weigh on the gods as well.

Note also a common theme in myths: the extremely beautiful male or female human (compare Narcissus and Psyche). Being of great beauty may suggest being closer to the gods. It also may cause fame, love--and tragedy.

Summary and Analysis of Cupid and Psyche

A stunningly beautiful girl, Psyche, is born after two older sisters. People throughout the land worship her beauty so deeply that they forget about the goddess Venus. Venus becomes angry that her temples are falling to ruin, so she plots to ruin Psyche. She instructs her son, Cupid, to pierce the girl with an arrow and make her fall in love with the most vile, hideous man alive. But when Cupid sees Psyche in her radiant glory, he shoots himself with the arrow instead.

Meanwhile, Psyche and her family become worried that she will never find a husband, for although men admire her beauty, they always seem content to marry someone else. Psyche's father prays to Apollo for help, and Apollo instructs her to go to the top of a hill, where she will marry not a man but a serpent. Psyche bravely follows the instructions and falls asleep on the hill. When she wakes up, she discovers a stunning mansion. Going inside, she relaxes and enjoys fine food and luxurious treatment. At night, in the dark, she meets and falls in love with her husband.

She lives happily with him, never seeing him, until one day he tells her that her sisters have been crying for her. She begs to see them, but her husband replies that it would not be wise to do so. Psyche insists that they visit, and when they do, they become extremely jealous of Psyche's beautiful mansion and lush quarters. They deduce that Psyche has never seen her husband, and they convince her that she must sneak a look. Confused and conflicted, Psyche turns on a lamp one night as her husband lies next to her.

When she sees the beautiful Cupid asleep on her bed, she weeps for her lack of faith. Cupid awakens and deserts her because Love cannot live where there is no trust. Cupid returns to his mother, Venus, who again decides to enact revenge on the beautiful girl.

Psyche, meanwhile, journeys all over the land to find Cupid. She decides to go to Venus herself in a plea for love and forgiveness, and when she finally sees Venus, the great goddess laughs aloud. Venus shows her a heap of seeds and tells her that she must sort them all in one night's time if she wants to see Cupid again. This task is impossible for one person alone, but ants pity Psyche and sort the seeds for her. Shocked, Venus then orders Psyche to sleep on the cold ground and eat only a piece of bread for dinner. But Psyche survives the night easily. Finally, Venus commands her to retrieve a golden fleece from the river. She almost drowns herself in the river because of her sorrow, but a reed speaks to her and suggests that she collect the golden pieces of fleece from the thorny briar that catches it. Psyche follows these instructions and returns a sizable quantity to Venus. The amazed goddess, still at it, now orders Psyche to fill a flask from the mouth of the River Styx. When Psyche reaches the head of the river, she realizes that this task seems impossible because the rocks are so dangerous. This time, an eagle helps her and fills the flask. Venus still does not give in. She challenges Psyche to go into the underworld and have Persephone put some of her beauty in a box. Miraculously, Psyche succeeds.

On her way toward giving the box to Venus, she becomes curious, opens the box, and instantly falls asleep. Meanwhile, Cupid looks for Psyche and finds her sleeping. He awakens her, puts the sleeping spell back in the box, and takes her to Zeus to request her immortality. Zeus grants the request and makes Psyche an immortal goddess. She and Cupid are married. Venus now supports the marriage because her son has married a goddess—and because Psyche will no longer distract the men on earth from Venus.

Analysis

This story centers on the power of true love. Psyche first doubts that love, feeling that she must see Cupid in the flesh. She later redeems herself many times over when she proves her commitment, overcoming all obstacles in her way. Figuratively, love (Cupid) and the soul ("psyche" is the Greek word for the soul) belong together in an inseparable union. When Cupid sees Psyche, the soul in its beauty, he immediately wants to join with her. Somehow, this beauty is admired by men but does not lead to the kind of love that eventuates in a marriage proposal. But Cupid is able to fully appreciate Psyche's beauty.

The happy ending, with Venus, Psyche, and Cupid all reaching a positive resolution, illustrates that when love is pure, all pains, sorrows, and challenges will align to ensure that the love is realized. Even nature, as the ants and eagle demonstrate, support true love. Of all the stories in the Greek mythology, none more clearly demonstrates that true love exists than this story. Moreover, Psyche reveals that true love is to be defended and supported no matter what the cost. This part of the myth is beautifully retold by the modern author C.S. Lewis under the title *Till We Have Faces*.

Psyche remains an unusual example of a female character who acts like a male hero. Although other female characters (such as Artemis) perform traditionally male activities, none so boldly acts as a hero might: overcoming seemingly impossible obstacles, fighting to win true love, achieving a status that is more than human.

Importantly, Psyche is a rare being who begins as a mortal and ends as a divinity. Her unique position raises questions about spirituality. Is the soul properly a thing of the earth or a thing of the heavens? How does Psyche's being change when she becomes immortal? Was there something about Psyche that was more than human from the very beginning, and why did she win the attention of Cupid in the first place?

The story continues to explore the distinction between humans and gods, as Venus is bitterly jealous of a mortal who draws other mortals away from her, a goddess. On earth, the soul, figured as Psyche, is amazingly beautiful but faces great trials. Order is restored when the soul reaches the heavens. The prospect of one's own soul following this path can be very attractive.

It seems that the decision is up to Zeus. Must a soul earn its place (with help) in the realm of divinity? Must there be an advocate, another god, who must bring the case to Zeus? Although such questions are left open, it seems clear that Psyche's determination, courage, and belief in true love help her achieve divine status.

This myth also shows some of the interlocking storylines of the myths. Psyche visits Persephone in the underworld (it must be winter). Persephone's box reminds us of Pandora's, especially because she is so curious to open it. We will see the River Styx again, too, not to mention Zeus and Venus. The interconnected nature of the tales does raise questions about chronology: besides the Creation of Earth, it is unclear what the chronology might be, and which story happens before another. But as the characters and places overlap, the myths show themselves to be not only intertextual with each other but also unified in their depiction of one world in which all these characters and stories exist.

Summary and Analysis of Pyramus and Thisbe; Orpheus and Eurydice; Ceyx and Alcyone; Pygmalion and Galetea

Pyramus and Thisbe are madly in love and live in houses next to each other. Their parents, however, forbid their romance and build a wall between the houses. The lovers find a chink in the wall through which they speak and kiss one another. One night they decide to run away together, meeting at the Tomb of Ninus. Thisbe arrives first, and she sees a terrifying lioness with blood on its mouth. She runs away in fear, dropping her cloak. The lioness tears up the cloak and bloodies it. When Pyramus arrives, he sees the cloak, assumes his lover has died, and kills himself in sorrow. Thisbe returns, sees Pyramus' body, and kills herself with the same knife. From then on, mulberries take on the dark red color of their blood, making the lovers' bond eternal.

...

Orpheus is the most talented musician alive, rivaling only the gods. He falls in love with Eurydice, but a viper stings her and she dies. Devastated, Orpheus travels down into the underworld to beg her return. He successfully charms the creatures of death with his sweet music, and finally Hades agrees to give Eurydice back to Orpheus on one condition: Orpheus must not look back at his wife as she follows him back above ground. Just before the two lovers return to the light, Orpheus cannot wait any longer and looks back. He sees his wife disappearing, saying "farewell."

...

Ceyx and Alcyone are married happily until the day when Ceyx decides to journey across the ocean. Knowing the dangers of the sea, Alcyone begs him not to go, or at least to take her with him. But Ceyx declines her offer and sets out without her. On the first night of the journey, a storm ravages his ship, and Ceyx dies with Alcyone's name on his lips. Alcyone continues to wait for her husband, making him cloaks and praying fruitlessly to Juno for his safe return. Juno pities the woman and asks Somnus, god of Sleep, to tell her the truth about her husband's death. Somnus sends his son Morpheus to break the news in a dream, so Morpheus takes the form of the drowned Ceyx. Alcyone wakes from the terrible dream and knows her husband has died. She goes into the ocean to drown herself and be with him, but she sees his body floating towards her. She dives in but, miraculously, flies over the waves instead of sinking into them. The gods have turned her into a bird! The body of Ceyx disappears, and Ceyx turns into a bird as well. They are still together, flying and in love.

...

Pygmalion is a tremendously talented artist who has never fallen in love with a woman. Instead, he has fallen in love with his art--specifically, a beautiful sculpture of a woman. He gives her presents, tucks her into bed, and dresses her. Finally, Pygmalion realizes the futility of his efforts and gives up. Venus notices the situation and pities him, turning the statue into a living woman named Galetea. Pygmalion marries her.

Analysis

Like the story of Cupid and Psyche, the myth of Pyramus and Thisbe centers around the idea that true love is forever. Love cannot be contained or regulated, even by death. Unlike with Cupid and Psyche, of course, this myth is a tragedy. The tale seems to be refigured in Shakespeare's Romeo and Juliet. Shakespeare certainly used this play in his Midsummer Night's Dream, in which the merchant characters stage their own version of the tragic love tale.

The tragedy that unfolds between Pyramus and Thisbe once again suggests that it is not the job of the gods to step in and make everything happy. Although they often take active rolls in helping human characters, they also may take a more passive role as observers. Pyramus and Thisbe seem to have done no wrong to any of the gods, but find themselves as victims to cruel fate.

The tragic myth of Orpheus and Eurydice concerns love and temptation. Orpheus overcomes enormous obstacles to win his love back, but in his desire he cannot withstand the temptation of looking back to make sure she is there. Like Psyche's need to see Cupid, Orpheus's need to see Eurydice marks a lack of trust or satisfaction in his situation. This myth emphasizes trust and faith in love, knowing that one's beloved is present and not needing to prove it.

As with Pyramus and Thisbe, Orpheus and Eurydice illustrate that lovers can meet tragic ends. Unlike Pyramus and Thisbe, however, Orpheus undoubtedly causes his own demise when he turns around to look at Eurydice. In this sense, the story highlights mankind's freewill. While fate clearly plays a strong role in most Greek myths, in this case it is unquestionably Orpheus's doubting which causes Eurydice' tragic farewell.

The story of Ceyx and Alcyone is an interesting variation on the Greek love myth because it is both tragic and hopeful. Although Ceyx has died and the two lovers will never have a human life together, the gods reward the lovers with new life as birds. The depth of passion and strength of commitment on Alcyone's part, at least, prove that the two mortals are worthy of everlasting life and love.

Note the gendered actions of Ceyx and Alcyone. Ceyx is the one who goes on the journey, while Alcyone stays home. She seems more concerned about being with him than with the dangers of the ocean—which are real. But Ceyx insists that he will travel without her.

Alcyone and Ceyx also illustrate the recurring theme of life's cycles. As in the story of Hyacinthus, when Apollo's love causes the slain man to return in the form of flowers, it is the love between Alcyone and Ceyx that allows them to move through life's cycle without death. In this way, they achieve a status somewhere between human and divine.

The famous myth of Pygmalion, often reinterpreted in modern times, is an unusual love story. Like the story of Narcissus, the tale of Pygmalion includes an unconventional romantic interest. If an artist's works are extensions of himself, Pygmalion's love for his art begins as a love for himself. In any case, a mortal loves a stone. Perhaps this is the analogue to a god loving a mortal.

It is only when Pygmalion leaves the sculpture alone that Venus intervenes. In this case, she does not seem jealous or threatened. Instead, she uses her power to increase love and to transform the stone to mortal status. Venus would draw the line, it seems, at any challenge to her divine prerogatives. The story thus rewards the recurring theme of humans using their rational intelligence. Although the love he feels for the sculpture is strong, Pygmalion finally relies upon his thinking mind to accept the impossibility of the affair. It is precisely when he does this that Venus turns the sculpture into a living woman, thus rewarding Pygmalion.

Finally, it is notable that so many myths are about a pair of persons, usually two males or a male and a female. This structure can help draw contrasts between competing qualities or show how similar qualities work together. More often, the pairing seems to reflect something about human relationships, focusing most intensely on the relationship between the two people.

Summary and Analysis of Baucis and Philemon; Endymion; Daphne; Alpheus and Arethusa

Jupiter and Mercury decide to test the hospitality of humans. They disguise themselves as poor travelers and knock on the doors of many houses, but no one will take them in. Finally they approach a small hut owned by Baucis and Philemon. The couple warmly invite the travelers inside and offer all their food and wine. Though it is not much, Baucis and Philemon explain that they are content with what they have because they love each other. Eventually, the gods reveal themselves. They destroy the rest of the town in a flood but spare Baucis and Philemon. Jupiter and Mercury also replace the hut with a large marble house. Baucis and Philemon ask the gods that when they die, they would like to die together. Many years later, in their old age, they are in the middle of a conversation when they notice leaves springing forth from their bodies. They turn into a conjoined tree—a linden and an oak both growing from one trunk.

...

A beautiful young man, Endymion, catches the attention of Selene, the Moon. Selene puts him in a magical slumber: he lies as if dead, but in fact he is alive and forever asleep. Every night, Selene covers him with kisses, but it is said that she still suffers from loneliness.

...

Daphne is a stunning wood nymph whom Apollo desires. He comes down and chases her through the woods, hoping to make her his own. Daphne, terrified, tries her best to outrun him. Just when he catches up to her, she screams for help from her father, and he turns her into a laurel tree. Though disappointed that he did not catch Daphne, Apollo decides that the laurel should be the victor's crown.

...

Arethusa, a mortal huntress, worships the speed and agility of Artemis. One day she is bathing in a river when she feels a rumbling beneath her. A voice says it is Alpheus, the river god, and the voice says that Alpheus loves her. But Arethusa wants nothing to do with him and runs away in fear. Just before Alpheus catches up to her, the huntress prays to Artemis. The goddess hears the prayer and turns Arethusa into a spring of water.

Analysis

Ovid notes that the myth of Baucis and Philemon shows not only that the gods exert great power on earth, but also that they reward the humble and the pious. They have appreciation for justice and piety. The myth also suggests that love does not necessarily depend on material wealth.

Baucis and Philemon also illustrate the recurring theme of true love. Unlike with Cupid and Psyche or many other love relationships, that between Baucis and Philemon is not particularly based on physical beauty. They are an older couple with a modest lifestyle, and they are hardly known through the land for their beauty. The story thus suggests that true love is humble and selfless. As with Ceyx and Alcyone, the love between Baucis and Philemon is rewarded as they become eternal trees. The use of natural imagery (common in Greek mythology) illustrates that true love exists naturally and beautifully. In this case, it is not hard to imagine something of the nature of love remaining in the transition from humans to entwined trees.

The short tale of Endymion suggests that the gods do not necessarily know how to successfully solve their problems. The Moon puts a sleep spell on the object of her desire, but this does not quench her desire for him. Being asleep, he is not much of a companion. Her action just increases her feeling of quiet solitude. Knowing this myth, we might look at the moon as a lonely being in the night sky, when most beings are asleep.

The myth of Daphne provides another example of a human becoming a plant. Unlike with Baucis and Philemon, however, Daphne becomes a plant in order to be saved from a god. Daphne's only choice in escaping what appears to be an impending rape is to become a tree. If Apollo cannot have her, he can at least declare that victors win parts of a laurel tree in the form of a crown. He thus retains some degree of control over Daphne, who is now a laurel herself.

Daphne provides an interesting contrast to Europa, who willingly went along with Zeus's pursuits. After Europa followed Zeus's orders, she went on to live a happy life in Crete and birth two children. Does following gods' orders always lead to a happier outcome? Does a person have no other choice than to do what she is told by a god?

The story of Alpheus and Arethusa appears to be a variation on the plot of Daphne and Apollo. The gods do sometimes look over and care for humans, even when they do so against other gods. The gods do play favorites.

Scholars cite this story as an example of female independence and power, for Arethusa effectively escapes from the river god with the help of a goddess. Yet again, however, Arethusa becomes water, just the thing over which Alpheus seems to have control.

Once again, natural imagery defines the tale. By connecting Alpheus to spring water, the story effectively places her in the reader's physical world. Spring water (just like hyacinth flowers or an echo) is invoked to remind readers of the tale and the moral it

Summary and Analysis of Baucis and Philemon; Endymion; Daph...

holds.

Summary and Analysis of Baucis and Philemon; Endymion; Daph...

Summary and Analysis of Phaethon; Pegasus and Bellerophon

Phaethon, a young man, travels to the Palace of the Sun to meet Apollo and find out if the sun god is in fact his father. Apollo says he is. To prove it, he will give Phaethon anything he wants, swearing by the River Styx that he will grant Phaethon his wildest dream. The boy's dream is to ride Apollo's chariot. Although his father warns him that no god (let alone a human) can control the horses and safely ride the chariot across the sky, Phaethon will not listen. Apollo seems to have no choice but to let his son drive the chariot and watch as the horses run recklessly through the sky, crashing into stars and even setting the earth on fire. To prevent the entire planet from burning, Zeus sends a thunderbolt which kills Phaethon and drives the horses into the sea.

...

In the city of Corinth, Glaucus is King. But the gods dislike him because he feeds his horses human flesh. Eventually the gods throw him from his chariot and have his horses eat him. It is thought that Glaucus's son is a beautiful young man named Bellerophon, but it is also rumored that the boy's father is Poseidon. More than anything, Bellerophon wants to ride Pegasus, a winged horse, so he goes to Athena's temple to pray. Athena comes to him in a dream and gives him a golden bridle which, she says, will tame the horse. It does, and Pegasus becomes Bellerophon's loyal beast.

Later, Bellerophon kills his brother entirely by accident. He goes to King Proteus for purification, which the king grants. But Bellerophon's situation becomes complicated when the king's wife takes an interest in him. Bellerophon denies the queen's advances, but the evil woman tells her husband that the boy has wronged her and must die. Proteus does not want to kill Bellerophon personally because the boy has eaten at his table, so instead he asks the boy to deliver a letter to the Lycian king.

On the back of Pegasus, Bellerophon travels easily, meets the Lycian king, and stays with him for nine wonderful days. When the king opens his letter, it has clear instructions to kill Bellerophon. But like Proteus, the Lycian king does not want to offend Zeus by acting violently towards a guest, so instead he sends Bellerophon on an impossible journey to kill a monster, Chimaera. With the help of Pegasus, however, Bellerophon kills the beast with no harm to himself. He returns to Proteus, and Proteus sends him on many more challenging adventures.

Eventually, the victorious Bellerophon wins Proteus's respect, and the king even gives the man his daughter's hand in marriage. Unfortunately, Bellerophon loses favor with the gods when he attempts to become more than human and take a place on Mount Olympus. When he tries to take the journey up to the gods' kingdom, Pegasus throws Bellerophon off his back. Bellerophon wanders alone, "devouring his own soul," until he dies. Pegasus becomes Zeus's favorite animal, residing in the stalls of Mount Olympus and bringing thunder and lightning to him.

Analysis

The tragic tale about Phaethon and his father perfectly explicates the dynamic between elders and youth. Apollo wants to do right by his son, but in meeting his son's heart's desire, he becomes the agent of his son's tragic death. He becomes helpless in the face of his son's brazen confidence. The myth teaches sons to be humble and reminds fathers that when they send their sons out into the world, it is normal to fear great dangers that their sons must face on their own. The instability caused by the deal between father and son ultimately requires the intervention of Zeus.

It is interesting that in this myth and in that of Bellerophon, there is a question about which son belongs to which father. This is a question that often is of interest to human beings, who cannot always be sure who is the father of a child. By what evidence can a father prove that he really is the father?

Once again, Zeus is associated with a natural element, the thunderbolt. In this story, the association of Zeus's power with lightning is quite clear--what natural element is more powerful than lightning? As in other stories, Zeus acts as an authority who must maintain order when no one else can. His decision to kill the young man reveals the god's rational mindset and priorities.

Wildly courageous and headstrong, Bellerophon is a complex hero. He seems to be close to godlike status, but Zeus puts him in his place at the end of the tale. As for Pegasus, it is a horse above horses. They are a good match. In both cases, they raise the recurring question of what separates humans from gods. The Greek heroes, such as Bellerophon, often achieve a status somewhere in between. Heroism clearly plays a role in the tale, as Bellerophon defeats Chimaera and performs seemingly impossible tasks. But unlike Hercules, Theseus, or Odysseus, Bellerophon loses favor with the gods at the end of the tale.

One interesting element in this tale is the ritual of hospitality. Neither king feels able to kill Bellerophon because the man has dined with him at the table, and it seems that the gods would punish a king who so poorly treated a guest. The other myth that most directly concerns hospitality is Baucis and Philemon, and in both tales the moral lesson is the same: hospitality is essential to win or keep divine favor.

The tale of Bellerophon also concerns a recurring theme in Greek mythology: a tragic mistake. Like Apollo, who accidentally kills Hyacinthus, Bellerophon kills his brother by mistake. It is interesting to note that the nature of the accident does not relieve him of his guilt: Bellerophon goes on his quest to achieve purity in order to win back the favor of the gods.

When pride emerges in this story, we see the disastrous effects it may have on a once heroic character. As he "devours his own soul," Bellerophon appears shockingly pathetic at the end of the story. After his amazing adventures, the gods have placed him in this state because of his egoism. The story thus serves as a warning against believing one is more than human.

Conversely, the tale reveals the rewards that come with dutiful prayer to the gods. Athena steps in to essentially save Bellerophon by giving him Pegasus, and she does so precisely because the young man has prayed at her temple. The gods seldom reveal themselves to be greatly eager to help humans for the humans' own sake, but in this case it seems clear that praying to her increased Bellerophon's chances.

Finally, the story of Bellerophon illustrates the important theme of loyalty. As soon as they team up, Pegasus is Bellerophon's dutiful beast and best friend. Like Prometheus and Io, the two make a connection that goes far beyond the differences in their natures. Although ultimately Pegasus (like the gods) rejects Bellerophon because of his egoism, the relationship illustrates the power and value of loyalty.

Summary and Analysis of Otus and Ephialtes; Daedalus

Otus and Ephialtes are enormous twins, sons of Poseidon. They think they are better than the gods and aggressively challenge them on several occasions. First, they kidnap Ares until the stealthy Hermes sets him free. Next they try to put one mountain on top of another. Just as Zeus is going to strike them down with a thunderbolt, Poseidon begs to save them and Zeus agrees. Finally, they try to capture Artemis, but the clever goddess runs away when she sees the twins. The twins chase her, even as she runs over water, until she disappears. In her place, Otus and Ephialtes see a beautiful white animal. They both throw spears at it, but it disappears as well, and the two spears hit the two giants instead. Artemis thus enacts revenge.

...

Daedalus is the brilliant architect who constructed the Labyrinth for the Minotaur in Crete. When King Minos learns that Theseus has escaped from it, he knows that Daedalus must have helped him out. As punishment, Minos puts Daedalus and his son Icarus in the Labyrinth. Even they cannot find a way out along the paths. Daedalus builds himself and his son wings out of wax and feathers. He warns Icarus not to fly too high because the sun will melt the wings. As they are flying in their escape, excitement and power overtake Icarus, and he flies too high. The sun melts his wings, the boy falls to the ocean, and the waters swallow him up.

Analysis

The myth of Otus and Ephialtes is a classic tale of egotism. Otus and Ephialtes lead the gods to reassert their supreme power by showing the surprising amount of power they have themselves. The two powerful giants engage in a rather effective rebellion, one more effective than many others in Greek mythology. Again, though, they fail. What is more, Artemis tricks and punishes them in the end.

As Artemis successfully takes revenge against the twins, she highlights the recurring theme that ingenuity is often more important than brute strength. That theme is made particularly clear through gender in this tale; a female character defeats two enormous, strong male characters. (At the same time, we cannot forget that the power of gods trumps the power of humans regardless of gender.)

The attempt to capture the beautiful goddess recalls the myths of Daphne and Arethusa. In this case, of course, the female character not only escapes the male but actually defeats him in the process.

The famous myth of Daedalus first highlights the recurring theme of human ingenuity. Daedalus knew how to make a Labyrinth and now figures out how to escape it. But the tale also illustrates the dangers of youthful arrogance. Like

Phaethon, Icarus disregards his father's advice and flies carelessly to his death.

The father/son relationship also comes to the forefront in the story of Daedalus. Like Apollo, who loves Phaethon but cannot save him from his youthful mistakes, Daedalus is rendered helpless in saving Icarus. For all his ingenuity, Daedalus cannot solve the generational problem that exists between him and his son. The son makes his own mistake, despite his father's advice, and suffers the consequences.

Summary and Analysis of Perseus

King Acrisius of Argos has a stunningly beautiful daughter but wants a son, so he prays to the gods. Apollo tells him not only that Acrisius will never have a son, but also that the son of his daughter will kill him. The only way to fully prevent this prophecy would be to kill his daughter, Danae, but Acrisius fears what the gods would do to him. Instead, he imprisons Danae in a bronze house without a roof and guards her carefully.

Arcisius does not expect, however, that Zeus will come to her and impregnate her. Perseus is born, and after Acrisius discovers the baby, he puts Perseus and Danae in a box and sets it out in the ocean. Luckily (or thanks to Zeus), the box washes up on a small island, where a kind fisherman named Dictys takes Danae and Perseus in. They live happily until Dictys's brother, King Polydectes, falls in love with Danae and decides to get rid of her son. Polydectes convinces Perseus to kill the Medusa, a horrifying beast with snakes for hair. But this feat seems impossible because whoever looks at the snakes will turn instantly to stone.

Hermes gives Perseus guidance and a sword stronger than the Medusa's scales. He tells Perseus that to fight the Medusa Perseus will need special equipment from the Nymphs of the North. Their location is a mystery, and Perseus must ask the Gray Women, three sisters who live in a gray land and are gray themselves. They share only one eye among the three, and they alternate using it. Before Perseus sets out to find them, Athena gives him her shield and tells him that he must look at the Medusa through the shield, like a mirror, in order to avoid turning to stone.

Perseus finds the Gray Women and steals the eyeball, holding it hostage in exchange for the location of the Nymphs of the North. Hermes helps Perseus travel there, where he finds a land of happy people, always banqueting and celebrating. They give him his three gifts: winged sandals, a magic wallet that changes to the size of whatever its contents, and, most important of all, a magic cap that will turn whoever wears it invisible.

With Hermes and Athena at his side, Perseus finds and kills Medusa. He puts the head in his wallet and flies, invisible, back toward his mother. On the way, he passes a beautiful woman chained to a rock, Andromeda, and falls in love with her instantly. She was chained there because her foolish mother had thought herself more beautiful than any goddess, so as punishment the gods told her to chain her daughter to a rock, where she would be eaten by a serpent. Perseus kills the serpent and takes Andromeda home.

When he returns to the island, he discovers that Danae and Dictys have gone into hiding because Danae will not marry Polydectes. The evil king, meanwhile, is hosting a banquet with all his supporters. Perseus barges in and holds up the head of Medusa. Unable to look away in time, all the men turn to stone. Perseus finds his mother, makes Dictys king, and marries Andromeda.

Optimistic, Perseus and Danae return to Argos to find her father, King Acrisius. They hope that his heart has warmed since he put them in a box out to sea, but when they reach Argos they realize that he fled the land. One day, Perseus competes in a discus-throwing contest. His disc veers far to the side and lands on a spectator in the crowd, killing him instantly. This is Acrisius, in fulfillment of Apollo's prophecy.

Analysis

This famous tale underscores the inescapable nature of fate and prophecies in the course of telling a hero's story. Although Acrisius took drastic action to change destiny, short of killing his own daughter he can do nothing to prevent his fate. Perseus is too strong to be kept down and on an island, so it is fitting that his fate is to go on adventures and quests and to be helped by gods. He fits the heroic model of an honorable man overcoming all obstacles to reunite his family and do justice.

It is interesting to note that the story does not indicate whether fate or Zeus guided Perseus's box to the island. As in the Creation of Earth, the reader must wonder who is in charge. Is there a difference between fate and Zeus, and if so, what is that boundary? Who controls Zeus's fate?

To the extent that Zeus does help Perseus, the story also illustrates the benefits that come with honorable behavior. Zeus, Hermes, and Athena all help Perseus at critical moments, allowing him to successfully complete his missions. Perseus, of course, contributes to his own success as well.

Hospitality again proves to be beloved by the gods: Dictys, the fisherman, becomes king. In this way, the story highlights that great people can have humble beginnings. Baucis and Philemon, the most clear examples of humble hospitality, share with Dictys a selflessness that ultimately the gods reward. The gods shower these humble characters with material wealth, but why? If humility and selflessness are important, why would physical wealth be the appropriate reward? Perhaps the answer lies in the context of such physical wealth and what it means to the characters.

As Perseus deals with the Gray Women, we see the imaginative nature of Greek mythology. These distinct characters, sharing one eye, all shades of gray, last in the reader's mind and expand the universe which the mythology depicts. Moreover, when Perseus actually defeats them, the story underscores the recurring theme of human ingenuity.

Perseus, of course, stands as a premiere example of Greek heroism. He overcomes all obstacles to defend his family and exact revenge. He proves honorable and valiant, calm and clever. As he fights for his mother's respect and hopes for his estranged father's love, he values family and loyalty above all else.

Medusa, by contrast, is one of the most famous mythical beings. In her case, it is not beauty but ugliness that causes problems for the observer. She is so terrible that one direct look at her turns a person to stone. Medusa is a direct contrast to the many beautiful characters (Adonis, Narcissus) who appear throughout the tales.

In this story, as in other tales of heroes, the Greek myths become adventure tales with unforgettable drama, high stakes, and imaginative characters. Such adventures and quests make eachstory live on throughout time as astounding literature that captures our imagination.

Summary and Analysis of Theseus

Theseus is the great Athenian hero. His father Aegeus is king of Athens, but Theseus grows up in southern Greece with his mother. When he is old enough, Theseus travels to the city to meet his father and overcomes many obstacles along the way. By the time he reaches Athens, he is known as a hero. Not realizing that Theseus is his son, King Aegeus is about to poison him, but just in time Theseus shows him a sword that his father left for him. Aegeus declares Theseus heir to the throne and sends him on an important journey.

Aegeus recounts the tragedy of Minos, the powerful ruler of Crete, who lost his only son Androgeus while the boy was in Athens. Aegeus had sent him on an expedition to kill a dangerous bull, but it killed Androgeus, and in revenge, King Minos vowed to destroy Athens unless every year seven maidens and seven men were sent to Crete. These sacrificial youth would be fed to the Minotaur, a monster, half-bull and half-human, who lived inside a labyrinth. Theseus comes forward to be offered as one of the victims. He promises his father that he will kill the Minotaur, and upon his successful return, his ship will carry a white sail.

When the fourteen men and women arrive in Crete, they are paraded through the town. Minos's daughter Ariadne sees and instantly falls in love with Theseus. She confers with Daedalus the architect to devise a plan for her beloved to stay safe. Then she meets with Theseus, who promises to marry her if he escapes from the labyrinth. Theseus follows Ariadne's plan, walking through the maze as he lets run a ball of string so he can retrace his steps. Theseus finds the Minotaur sleeping and kills it with his bare hands. Theseus, Ariadne, and the other Athenian youth all escape to the ship going back to Athens.

On the way back, Ariadne dies. Some say Theseus deserted her on an island. Others say he let her rest on an island because she was seasick, then got caught in a storm, and by the time he returned to the island she was dead. In any case, for some reason Theseus forgets to raise the white sail. His father, seeing the black sail, assumes his son has died and jumps into the sea. The sea has been called the Aegean ever since.

Theseus rules in a people-friendly fashion, and Athens becomes the happiest city in the world. In later years, however, sadness ensues after he marries Ariadne's sister Phaedra. Theseus already had a child, Hippolytus. When Theseus and Phaedra visit him, Phaedra falls madly in love with Hippolytus, her stepson. He refuses her advances, but she writes a letter falsely alleging that he violated her, and then she kills herself. Theseus finds the letter and banishes his innocent son. Artemis appears to Theseus and reveals the truth, but it is too late because the boy has already been killed at sea.

Analysis

The story of Theseus is one of the most famous tales of Greek mythology. Indeed, Theseus is one of the best examples of a Greek hero. Not only does he use cunning and strength to kill the Minotaur, but he also works to reunite his family and his kingdom. He goes on to become a monarch who serves his people well. This myth also illuminates the perception that Athens was, in its day, the most respected and just land. The government of justice that Theseus oversaw became an idealized model for Greek and Roman culture throughout history.

The story's tragic end, however, suggests the fragility of goodness and mortal happiness even for a hero like Theseus. Like Bellerophon, he becomes a more complex character as the end of his life becomes more complex than its clearly heroic beginnings. Between Ariadne's death, Aegeus's suicide, and the Phaedra tragedy, Theseus becomes a complicated figure who outgrows his earlier, simpler role of hero.

The tale of Phaedra and Hippolytus may illustrate some of the gendered power relations in ancient Greek life. It was reasonable to imagine that a woman at that time might kill herself after being raped. Phaedra takes advantage of that expectation in revenge, being so distraught over her failure to seduce Hippolytus that she is willing both to kill herself and to ruin his life. Contrast this relationship to that of Theseus and Ariadne; without her, he could not have escaped the labyrinth.

Indeed, the relationship between Ariadne and Theseus is an interesting one as it speaks to the recurring theme of true love. Although in the beginning it seems as if these two lovers have found the true love that the gods support, Hamilton puts that idea into doubt when she reports the idea that Theseus may have left her on an island to die. Although such an action would seem out of place for his character, the alternative suggestion is that Ariadne died because he left her on an island for too long. When he marries her sister, tragic events unfold, and it seems that fate did not look happily on the affair. True love, it seems, is not simple at all--it can cause all kinds of trouble and lead to all kinds of quests and adventures.

The tragedy of Aegeus brings up the recurring theme of a tragic mistake. When Theseus forgets to raise the correct flag, his carelessness takes a fatal turn against someone he loves. Like Apollo killing his best friend Hyacinthus, Theseus clearly means well but makes a tragic mistake. Unlike the other fathers who lose sons, Aegeus is so distraught that he chooses to die himself.

Like the story of Perseus, the tales of Theseus take on an adventurous tone with epic proportions. From the Labyrinth to the Minotaur, Ariadne to Aegeus, the tales of Theseus have become iconic in the Western canon.

Summary and Analysis of Theseus

Summary and Analysis of Hercules; Atalanta

Hercules is considered the greatest Greek hero of all. Unlike Theseus, who was both very strong and thoughtful, Hercules simply is strong. In fact, he is the strongest man who has ever existed, and therefore he considers himself something of a god. Indeed, he is half-god, a son of Zeus. Supremely confident, Hercules showed his brute force from a very early age, when he wrestled a snake that had slithered into his baby cradle.

The saddest incident of his life occurs after he has married Princess Megara and had three children with her. Hera, Zeus's jealous wife, cannot forgive her husband for having had Hercules as an illicit son, so she sends Hercules into insanity. One night Hercules goes mad and unwittingly kills his three boys. When he realizes what he has done, he almost kills himself, but Theseus persuades him to go on living; that is the heroic option.

To cleanse himself, Hercules visits the Oracle at Delphi. The Oracle tells him to go to Eurystheus, who sends him on almost impossible challenges. Hercules completes all of his twelve labors: killing the lion of Nemea, killing a creature with nine heads called the Hydra, capturing a stag with horns of gold, killing a boar, cleaning the thousands of Aegean stables in one day, exiling the Stymphalian birds, going to Crete and retrieving the beautiful savage bull that Poseidon gave Minos, retrieving the man-eating mares, bringing back the girdle of Hippolyta, returning the back of the cattle of Geryon (a monster with three bodies), bringing back the Golden Apples of Hesperides—and, finally, bringing Cerberus, the three-headed dog, up from Hades.

...

When Atalanta's father sees that his child is a girl, not a boy, he leaves the poor infant on a mountaintop to die. Luckily for her, a she-bear discovers her and raises her to become a fast, daring young woman. She builds a reputation for being the best huntress in the land and becomes famous for killing a ruthless boar. Of all her adventures, the story of the golden apple is most famous. Atalanta decrees that she will marry whichever suitor can outrun her in a race. Knowing that she is faster than everyone, Atalanta smugly beats them all to the finish line.

But one man, named Hippomenes, gets three exquisite golden apples. Along the race, the suitor drops one apple at a time. Atalanta cannot resist stopping to pick them up, and to her surprise, the suitor wins the race. She makes good on the vow and becomes his wife.

Analysis

Hercules, one of the most famous Greek figures, shares a trouble with Theseus, for both men inadvertently kill their sons. For Hercules, justice means engaging in a series of feats of strength that almost no mortal could accomplish. Psychologically, it makes sense that Hercules would look for wisdom at such a time from the Oracle and that he would face his demons by engaging in endless trials of his virtue. Of course, his incredible strength and superhuman power secure his place in legend. Nonetheless, his need for purification, which draws him into action, is at its core a human rather than a divine aspect of his being.

Moreover, his acts of purification align him more closely with Bellerophon, who killed his brother by accident. In both of these situations, the hero's good will does not affect his wrong actions. In the case of Hercules, who kills his children simply because Hera puts a spell on him, the tragic killings appear especially unfair. Why should Hercules be punished for crimes he committed because of Hera's manipulation? In the way he accepts his fate and seeks purification, Hercules proves himself to be humble in the way that Greek culture promoted.

Like the myths about Theseus, Perseus, and Bellerophon, the tales of Hercules combine high adventure with unforgettable characters. The stories remain classic examples of the incredible story-telling techniques of the Greek myths.

Juxtaposed with the extreme strength of Hercules is the extreme speed of Atalanta. She fails in one of her labors, however; ingenuity beats speed in her final race. The temptation of a beautiful apple slows the woman down (compare Eve in *Genesis*). Despite this trickery, however, Atalanta is still faster than Hippomenes and all the other men. Still, the lesson here is that a person has been foiled by her own greed; without this important character flaw, the trick would not have worked.

The theme of competition also is clear in the story of Atalanta. As in other myths, the competition serves as a narrative climax to the story. Indeed, Atalanta imbues the race with great importance: her romantic future, the lives of her competitors, and her impressive athletic reputation all are on the line. A competition in physical prowess demonstrates who has the most physical virtue and deserves honor in the society.

The story also underscores the importance of fate. Although Atalanta's father leaves her for dead in the woods, he cannot keep the she-bear from raising her as one of her own. As we have seen in several other stories (Io and Prometheus, Bellerophon and Pegasus), the relationship between Atalanta and a she-bear marks a strong connection between an animal and a human. Again, this theme suggests a connection between the natural world and the human spirit.

Summary and Analysis of The Quest for the Golden Fleece

A Greek king, Athamas, gets tired of his wife Nephele and puts her jail. He marries Io, a young princess, in her place. Nephele prays that Io will not kill her two children in order to make Io's own children inherit the kingdom. Io does attempt this murder, however. She secretly gathers seed-corn and parches the seed so that no crops will grow. Then, when Athamas asks for word from an oracle about how to end the famine, Io bribes a messenger to say that the only way to bring back the crops is to sacrifice his son, Phrixus. Athamus and Io bring the boy to the sacrificial altar, but just before the murder, a wondrous ram with a golden fleece takes the boy and his sister and runs away. The ram, sent by Hermes, is an answer to Nephele's prayers.

The ram carries the children across the water from Europe to Asia, and on the way, the girl slips off and drowns. Phrixus arrives safely in the country of Colchis, where he sacrifices the ram and gives it to King Etes.

Meanwhile, in another part of Greece, a king named Pelias has stolen the crown from his brother. An oracle tells him that he will die at the hands of a kinsman and that he should be wary of a man wearing only one sandal. One day, a man wearing one sandal comes to town. This is Jason, the king's nephew, come to claim his rightful place as king. Pelias tells Jason that he would give up the throne if Jason would go out and retrieve the golden fleece. Jason sets off and overcomes many obstacles and adventures on the way to Colchis. Finally, with the help of Hera, he reaches King Etes.

Hera and Aphrodite arrange for Cupid to make King Etes's daughter, Medea, fall in love with Jason. Jason asks Etes for the fleece, but Etes says Jason must plow a field of dragon's teeth, which will spring up into a crop of armed men who must be cut down as they advance and attack. Jason agrees, though he believes the task will result in his death. Thanks to Cupid's bow, however, Medea gives Jason a magical potion that gives give him invincibility for one day. She also tells him to throw a rock into the middle of the army because it will lead the armed men to kill each other. The next day, Jason proves victorious.

The treacherous king will not give him the fleece, however. He plans to kill Jason. Medea helps him again. She leads him to the fleece, charms the serpent guarding it, and flees with Jason back home.

On the journey home, Medea kills her brother in the idea that she is protecting Jason. This is the first sign of her madness. When they return to Greece, she arranges for King Pelias to be killed by his own daughters, which fulfills the oracle. Later, Jason marries another woman, and Medea becomes so angry that she kills both the bride and her own two sons fathered by Jason.

Analysis

The story of the Quest for the Golden Fleece highlights the dangers of selfishness and jealousy. King Athamas, King Pelias, and Media all drive the people around them (and themselves) into chaos as a result of their self-serving motives. The story also reveals complex family loyalties. Various family members are jealous of outsiders and other insiders, and they are willing to kill to achieve their goals. Medea arranges for Pelias to be killed by his own daughters. Later, she kills her own children and Jason's new bride to exact revenge. Io attempts to kill Nephele's children.

In other instances, characters go out of their way to save people in their families. Medea kills her own brothers to protect Jason, wisely or not. Nephele prays to Hermes to save her children. In all of these situations, family loyalties are as strong as they are complex. Only Jason and Nephele appear to have purely ethical intentions and clear loyalties.

The human sacrifice is interrupted by the ram with the golden fleece (compare the story of Abraham and Isaac in *Genesis* and some versions of the Greek myth of Iphigenia). Instead of taking the place of the ones to be sacrificed, this ram escapes along with them. The fleece of the ram seems to hold special redemptive power. It becomes an almost magical item worthy of a quest. In order to retrieve it, Jason needs the help of Medea as well as some magic and divine help.

Medea first proves selfless in helping Jason win the golden fleece, but she eventually crosses a mental boundary and acts unforgivably. This mad selfishness, made worse by jealousy, reveals some psychological depth in her character. Throughout Western literature and theater, she stands as an unforgettable example of the duality in human nature, the combination of the rational and the irrational, as well as an example of the horrifying consequences of jealousy.

As in other stories, the gods involve themselves in human affairs to effect the outcome they perceive as positive. As with Bellerophon and Theseus, they support Jason, the hero, in his noble quest to defend his family and his position as king. The gods also answer Nephele's prayers, which underscores the recurring theme that the gods sometimes listen to humans.

Summary and Analysis of Tantalus and Niobe; Iphigenia Among the Taurians

Tantalus is a son of Zeus who is extremely well-liked by the gods until he plays a malicious trick. He murders his son Pelops and tries to feed Pelops to the gods without their knowledge. Of course, they all see through the trick. As punishment, they put Tantalus in Hades in a pool full of water. But the water always recedes as he tries to drink from it. Similarly, trees above him bear beautiful fruit, but the instant he reaches for them, they recede. Thus "tantalized," Tantalus will neither drink nor eat for eternity.

The gods also bring Pelops back to life. He has a daughter, Niobe. Like Tantalus, Niobe believes herself to be better than the gods. As a queen with seven strong sons and seven beautiful daughters, Niobe feels superior to the goddess Leto, and she tells her subjects to worship her instead of Leto. But Artemis and Apollo shoot deadly arrows into Niobe's fourteen children. Niobe cries until she turns into a stone that is always covered with tears, night and day.

...

Greek hunters kill one of Artemis's favorite wild animals. To win back her affection, they must sacrifice a young girl, Iphigenia. Just as the knife falls on her neck, however, she disappears. In this version of the tale, Athena has relocated the girl to the land of the Taurians. Iphigenia is made queen and forced to arrange the death of any Greek person who happens upon the island. She is very depressed and misses home for a long time.

One day, Iphigenia's younger brother Orestes and his friend Pylades arrive. Orestes accidentally killed his mother, and in order to cleanse himself, the gods told him, he must go to the land of the Taurians. Wracked with guilt, Oretes assumed he would meet his death on the island. Indeed, Iphigenia almost kills him, but just in time they realize their kinship, and they escape the island together.

Unfortunately, wind blows their ship back to land. The king almost kills his treacherous wife and her brother, but Athena steps in and, with the help of Poseidon, arranges for their safe travel.

Analysis

In the stories of both Tantalus and Niobe, the gods do not tolerate challenges from mortals. The harsh punishment dealt to both characters serves as a reminder that humans should never try to put themselves on the level of or even ahead of the gods. The punishment for Tantalus is fitting in that his crime also involved eating. Leto's punishment is to lose her children, who were central to her pride. Tantalus deserves special punishment for being a father who kills his own son, unlike the other fathers in almost all the other myths.

The harsh punishment of the gods shows that they have no mercy in dealing punishment to such egoists. The image of Artemis murdering all of Niobe's children stands out as a particularly vivid display of divine superiority. The theme of human and godly status recurs throughout the Greek myths, but nowhere is it more clear that the gods do not appreciate any human believing himself to be more than he is.

The stories of Tantalus and Niobe reveal the interconnected nature of the tales, as Niobe is Tantalus's granddaughter. Does such egoism run in the family? Why are two characters, separated by two generations, so very similar to one another? The parallels between the characters are too clear to ignore.

Hamilton's version of the myth of Iphigenia displays the power of familial loyalty as well as the willingness of gods sometimes to protect humans. Twice in the tale, Athena steps in at the last moment to directly alter Iphigenia's fate. Iphigenia was innocent from the start, and perhaps she cannot be faulted for wanting to escape the island. But indeed she is guilty of trying to escape and of failing to kill her brother according to the law of the Taurians. Whether Iphigenia is truly guilty or innocent, Athena brings her justice to the situation.

As for family loyalties, Iphigenia reveals that no bond is more powerful than that which she feels for her brother. Orestes, who accidentally killed his mother, also feels the importance of family loyalty. Similarly, the recurring theme of the tragic mistake arises again in this tale. Since the gods do help the brother and sister, it seems that there may be a measure of forgiveness for innocent but tragic acts. Perhaps because Orestes assumed he would meet his death on the desert island, the gods took pity on him. In any case, the family bond between brother and sister remains intact despite all other circumstances.

Summary and Analysis of Oedipus; Antigone

King Laius of Thebes hears from the Oracle at Delphi that he will die at the hands of his own son. To prevent this from happening, he leaves his baby boy on a mountain for dead, but another man saves the baby. Years later, Laius is murdered by robbers on the road.

At the same time, a huge Sphinx has been terrorizing the land. One man, Oedipus, comes upon it on the road. Oedipus has been running away from home because an oracle has predicted he will kill his father. The Sphinx gives him an unsolved riddle: what creature walks on four legs, then two, then three? Oedipus answers: mankind, who crawls, then walks, then uses a cane. This answer is correct, and the Sphinx kills itself. Oedipus becomes a famous liberator and marries the late king's wife, Jocasta.

After years of happy rule, a terrible plague hits the land. An oracle decrees that the only way for the plague to end would be to punish King Laius's killer. Oedipus seeks the truth, but a prophet tells Oedipus that he himself is the killer. A man from the robbery of Laius says the same thing. Upon realizing this truth, it becomes clear to Oedipus that he has killed his father and then married his own mother. Jocasta kills herself, and Oedipus pokes out his eyes, both people feeling immense shame and guilt.

Oedipus and his wife/mother Jocasta have several daughters and sons. After the horrific truth came out that Oedipus killed his father and married his mother, Oedipus exiled himself to an island where his daughter Antigone takes care of him until he dies.

Back in Thebes, Jocasta's brother, Creon, becomes king, but Oedipus's son Polyneices wages war against him. Oedipus's other son Eteocles defends Thebes, and in the fighting, the two brothers kill each other. With his power unchallenged, Creon declares that no one should bury Polyneices, but in Greek culture, the process of burying the dead is very sacred in order to give the soul happiness in the afterlife. In secret, Antigone buries her brother, so Creon kills her for her noble crime.

Analysis

The famous tales of Oedipus compel us most of all in how Oedipus comes to realize the awful fulfillment of the prophecies and the true circumstances of his fate. Though he is wise enough to beat the Sphinx, his unrelenting search for the truth (in order to help his city recover from the plague) leads to his ruin. Both King Laius and Oedipus attempted to subvert the prophecies, but they both acted out their common fate after all. Free will remains circumscribed by fate, suggesting that humans are bound to a destiny regardless of their choices. Knowledge of the truth proves to be an awful condition for those who have committed great sins.

A recurring theme in Greek mythology is that of guilt and innocence. We have seen how tragic mistakes do not render characters innocent of the crimes they commit. Similarly, Oedipus is guilty for his actions, even though he did not know that he was killing his father and marrying his mother. This story, like the others, raises the question: how can humans be blamed for actions they do not fully understand? As the characters try to purify themselves, will they ever find justice?

This myth has taken a special spin since the time of Sigmund Freud, who famously suggested that the simultaneous attractive and revolting power of the myth is not so much about the dangers of truth and knowledge but about the prospect of understanding that boys are fundamentally and unconsciously in love with their mothers and therefore in deathly competition with their fathers.

Antigone is a model of honor and sacrifice for the sake of familial loyalty. She cares for her bereft and guilt-ridden father, and then she insists on burying her slain brother in the face of an unjust law and likely death. The tragedy does not depict a reward for her valor, but readers appreciate (or at least debate) her honorable actions. The gods and magical items are not significant players in this political and social drama; the focus is on Antigone and her moral choices.

The theme of family loyalty arises throughout the Greek myths, but in this story, we see how far a character will go to defend it. Other times someone has died or risked death for a family member or a lover; Antigone acts in a way similar to Theseus, Perseus, and Bellerophon. Her actions do not take her on wild adventures, like these other heroes, but she does achieve a heroic, sacrificial status nonetheless. The Greek myths clearly support family loyalty, and this tale stands as a prime example of how the stories were used to convey moral messages.

This myth also brings the myths rather far from the tales of gods into the world of human culture and politics. Antigone is caught up in the middle of political and ethical battles fought on human terms and in light of competing human values.

Suggested Essay Questions

1. What role does pride play in Greek mythology?

   Answer: Specific characters illustrate the difference between confidence and egotism. A hero is confident in his strength, but pride goes too far when a human challenges the gods. Pride cometh before a fall.

2. How do the myths differentiate between human and divine power?

   Answer: Many of the myths point out these distinctions. The gods intervene when humans need help or when the gods want to accomplish goals on earth, but humans are often unable to solve their own problems and cannot really intervene among the gods; mortals even have limited abilities in the Underworld. When a human asserts divine power, the gods often put the person back in his or her place.

3. What do the Greek myths suggest about tragedy?

   Answer: Tragedy serves both as a narrative device and as a reminder of everyday human reality. In tale after tale, tragedy unfolds. Even some stories that begin happily have unexpected, sad endings for their characters. Human failings, prophecies, and unexpected coincidences all can lead to tragedy.

4. How is the value of family loyalty portrayed by the myths?

   Answer: Many of the Greek myths center around the importance of family relationships. Although some family members kill one another, the family members who show loyalty tend to be set up for admiration. Antigone, for instance, challenges the law of Creon in order to bury her brother, facing death rather than be disloyal to her brother. Yet, loyalty is not so uncomplicated; her two brothers had fought on opposite sides in the conflict. Loyalty to one's family is complicated by conflicts even within one's family.

5. How does the conflict between free will and the predestination of fate play out in Greek mythology?

   Answer: Free will appears to be circumscribed by fate. Despite our best efforts, fate controls our destiny. On the level of individual decisions, however, humans make their own choices and face the consequences. Human nature is implicated here: it seems that we all are fated to die, yet we have much we may choose to do while we are alive.

6. What have the myths to tell us about love?

   Answer: Many different human relationships can be characterized by love: family love, the love of friends, and romantic love all lead people to do things with and for their beloveds that they would not otherwise do to the point of great feats of skill and strength, on the one hand, or murder on the other hand. The gods sometimes love one another in similar ways. When gods and humans love one another, complications often ensue. When love is one-sided, moreover, other complications ensue. Cupid can make people fall in love, or people can fall instantly in love with one another.

7. How do myths account for natural events?

Answer: To account for something in nature that people do not yet understand, they tell a story about a being whose actions or life has resulted in what can be observed. Sometimes the story seems to have nothing in common with the reality that scientists later construct as explanation, but sometimes elements of the story are good metaphors for details of the natural event.

8. What is Greek virtue in the Greek myths?

Answer: We most often see virtue displayed by the Greek heroes, although we need not see all of their choices and actions as virtuous. Male virtue and female virtue seem to be different, but all virtue seems to have in common something about greatness, whether it is about wisdom, mental cunning, physical strength or speed, loyalty, or love. The characters who are honored by the gods appear to be the ones with virtue or who made virtuous choices, such as those who engaged in hospitality, while those who are punished by the gods appear to have either abused their virtue or contaminated it with pride. But the gods also test those whom they admire for their virtue, or even punish sometimes out of jealousy.

9. How do the Greek myths fit together?

Answer: Sometimes they do, and often they do not. Sometimes a myth picks up where another left off. Sometimes a myth expands upon a neglected but interesting part of another myth. The myths are told and retold with different emphases at different points in history and from the perspectives of different tellers. But they all tell a story of a hierarchy of gods, humans, and nature in which problems arise and choices must be made.

10. Why do so many beings transform in the myths?

Answer: In the myths about nature, we see something human in nature when we imagine that a transformation has taken place, such as when a hyacinth can be traced to Hyacinthus. Indeed, in a world where scientific explanations are difficult, it is not uncommon to imagine that one being simply turns into another. In a world before science and evolution, transformations occur quickly, and the boundaries between stone, plants, animals, people, and gods seem easy to cross with the power of the gods. From a narrative point of view, the plot can move faster if one being simply becomes another being able to accomplish what is needed for the tale. An interesting question to consider in each transformation is how much of the original nature, if any, is preserved after the change.

What Is True about a Myth?

When people first encounter myths at a young age, they often sense that something is true about them. As they learn more about the world, people realize that the myths they grew up with are not literally true. But the myths very often turn out to hold truth metaphorically. The myths are early literature, and like other literature they tell truth in a mode that philosophy and science cannot, since they embody the truth through accounts of specific living beings. Some topics, such as love and family relationships, are perhaps more truly explained through this mode and the perspective of specific individuals.

Another way of explaining this point is to say that literature and philosophy need one another to provide full explanations of human experience. On such points, see Martha Nussbaum's excellent book *Love's Knowledge*. People tell stories all the time because stories are meaningful ways to get across the realities of human experience. If we were to insist that no one may give credence to anything not given in the terms of science and logic, our discourse would be greatly impoverished.

If Freud is right, myths like that of Oedipus express what is normally inexpressible about the human condition, such as the young child's feelings about his parents. The most unlikely scenario may turn out to be generally true about us, if we only let ourselves encounter the inexpressible and face the taboo. On a more mundane level, most everyone can understand the feelings of family members who grieve over the loss of a parent, sibling, or child, and there is a sense in which the extreme reactions of these family members reflect the truth of what grieving persons might really want to do, even if, in a saner moment, they never would choose to take their grief to an extreme.

Even the mythical accounts of nature express a sort of truth. Winter's dark and cold months are expressed well in the myth of Persephone, whether or not she is really in the Underworld and Demeter is grieving. Yes, we know already that winter is this way, at least at Greek latitudes, but that does not make the myth less true in the telling. Likewise, that echoes exist is true, and whether or not we have ever heard an echo across a canyon, the myth tells us something we truly can expect about nature.

There is much that is false about myths and about all fiction by nature. There is a famous ancient quarrel between philosophers and poets. Nevertheless, we would not be reading the myths today if they had nothing lasting to offer us.

What Is True about a Myth?

Author of ClassicNote and Sources

Stephen Haskell, author of ClassicNote. Completed on January 19, 2008, copyright held by GradeSaver.

Updated and revised Adam Kissel May 28, 2008. Copyright held by GradeSaver.

Bernard Evslin. Heroes, Gods and Monsters of the Greek Myths. Chicago: Laurel Leaf, 1984.

Robert J. Lenardon and Mark P. O. Morford. Classical Mythology. New York: Oxford University Press, 2006.

Richard P. Martin. Myths of the Ancient Greeks. New York: NAL Trade, 2003.

Barry Powell. Classical Myth: Fifth Edition. New York: Prentice Hall, 2006.

"Greek Mythology." 2008-02-29. <http://www.mythweb.com/>.

"Living Myths." 2008-02-29. <http://www.livingmyths.com/Greek.htm>.

"Greek Mythology." 2008-02-29. <http://messagenet.com/myths/>.

"Greek Mythology." 2008-02-29.
<http://www.desy.de/gna/interpedia/greek_myth/greek_myth.html>.

"Greek Myths and Legends." 2008-02-29.
<http://atschool.eduweb.co.uk/carolrb/greek/greek1.html>.

Quiz 1

1. **How does Odysseus make Polyphemus fall asleep?**
    A. Gives him a sleeping potion
    B. Gives him wine
    C. Asks Hera for help
    D. Sings a song

2. **How do Odysseus's men escape Polyphemus's cave?**
    A. By hiding under the bellies of rams
    B. By sneaking out when Polyphemus is asleep
    C. By wearing sheepskins
    D. By walking out at night, in the dark

3. **Nemesis is the god of what?**
    A. Regret
    B. Disgust
    C. Rivalry
    D. Anger

4. **Why did the gods make Narcissus fall in love with his own reflection?**
    A. He never returned the affections of anyone else
    B. Narcissus thought himself better than the gods
    C. Cupid's arrow hit him as he looked at himself
    D. Hera was jealous of Echo

5. **Who does Hera punish for being an object of Zeus's desire?**
    A. Psyche
    B. Alcyone
    C. Echo
    D. Persephone

6. **Who did Apollo kill?**
    A. Adonis
    B. Otus
    C. Hyacinthus
    D. Polyphemus

7. **Who won the attention of both Aphrodite and Persephone?**
   A. Adonis
   B. Hermes
   C. Hercules
   D. Narcissus

8. **How did Adonis die?**
   A. Punishment from Zeus
   B. Killed by his own father
   C. Killed by a wild boar
   D. Old age

9. **Whom did Cupid himself fall in love with?**
   A. Thisbe
   B. Psyche
   C. Niobe
   D. Venus

10. **Who tried to ruin Psyche for being so beautiful?**
    A. Europa
    B. Artemis
    C. Hera
    D. Venus

11. **Psyche's father was told that his daughter would marry**
    A. Apollo
    B. A serpent
    C. Cupid
    D. No one

12. **Psyche gave Venus a golden fleece by**
    A. Collecting pieces of fleece from a thorny briar
    B. Marrying Cupid
    C. Begging Jason for help
    D. Capturing it from King Etes

13. **When Psyche opened the box Persephone gave her, what happened?**
    A. She found a magic seed
    B. She became queen of the underworld
    C. She unleashed all the negative thoughts and ideas of the world
    D. She fell asleep

14. **Who helped Psyche fill her flask from the River Styx?**
    A. An eagle
    B. Persephone
    C. Hades
    D. A hawk

15. **Where did Pyramus and Thisbe plan to meet upon their escape?**
    A. Under a bridge
    B. In a cave
    C. At the apothecary's store
    D. Ninus's tomb

16. **What became a symbol of Pyramus and Thisbe's tragic love?**
    A. Pomegranates
    B. Red wine
    C. The lily
    D. Mulberries

17. **How did Orpheus charm the creatures of the underworld?**
    A. With his pleas
    B. With his music
    C. With his poetry
    D. With his good looks

18. **How did Eurydice die?**
    A. Drowned
    B. Stung by a viper
    C. Pricked by a poisonous needle
    D. Ate a bad mushroom

19. **What was the condition upon which Orpheus could save Eurydice?**
    A. He could not look back at her as they left the underworld
    B. He could never sing again
    C. She could not speak
    D. She would have to return for half of every year

20. **How did Ceyx and Alcyone achieve immortality?**
    A. They return every spring in the form of flowers
    B. They became birds that still fly together
    C. They became mulberries
    D. They became gods on Mount Olympus

21. **Who told Alcyone her husband had died?**
    A. Morpheus
    B. Ceyx
    C. Juno
    D. Hades

22. **How did Ceyx die?**
    A. Jumping into the sea
    B. At Ninus's tomb
    C. At sea, in a storm
    D. In his sleep

23. **Who took pity on Pygmalion?**
    A. Galetea
    B. Zeus
    C. Cupid
    D. Venus

24. **Whom did Pygmalion marry?**
    A. Galetea
    B. Eurydice
    C. A sculpture
    D. No one

25. **What did Baucis and Philemon become when they died?**
  A. Flowers
  B. A conjoined tree
  C. Birds
  D. Raspberries

Quiz 1 Answer Key

1. **(B)** Gives him wine
2. **(A)** By hiding under the bellies of rams
3. **(D)** Anger
4. **(A)** He never returned the affections of anyone else
5. **(C)** Echo
6. **(C)** Hyacinthus
7. **(A)** Adonis
8. **(C)** Killed by a wild boar
9. **(B)** Psyche
10. **(D)** Venus
11. **(B)** A serpent
12. **(A)** Collecting pieces of fleece from a thorny briar
13. **(D)** She fell asleep
14. **(A)** An eagle
15. **(D)** Ninus's tomb
16. **(D)** Mulberries
17. **(B)** With his music
18. **(B)** Stung by a viper
19. **(A)** He could not look back at her as they left the underworld
20. **(B)** They became birds that still fly together
21. **(A)** Morpheus
22. **(C)** At sea, in a storm
23. **(D)** Venus
24. **(A)** Galetea
25. **(B)** A conjoined tree

Quiz 2

1. **What was Baucis's and Philemon's wish for the gods?**
   - A. That the gods be merciful on victims of the flood
   - B. That when they die, they die together
   - C. That they live forever
   - D. That they live in a large marble house

2. **Who are good examples of generosity?**
   - A. Cupid and Psyche
   - B. Tantalus and Niobe
   - C. Pyramus and Thisbe
   - D. Baucis and Philemon

3. **Who fell in love with Endymion?**
   - A. Selene
   - B. Aphrodite
   - C. Hera
   - D. Venus

4. **What is Endymion's magical spell?**
   - A. He will sleep forever
   - B. He has an enhanced sense of smell but cannot touch
   - C. He cannot speak unless spoken to
   - D. He can only repeat what others say

5. **What did Daphne turn into?**
   - A. An oak tree
   - B. A rose bush
   - C. A linden tree
   - D. A laurel tree

6. **Who chased Daphne through the woods?**
   - A. Apollo
   - B. Phaethon
   - C. Zeus
   - D. Prometheus

7. **What did Arethusa turn into?**
   A. A pomegranate
   B. A spring of water
   C. A rose bush
   D. A linden tree

8. **Who was Arethusa's favorite god or goddess?**
   A. Alpheus
   B. Artemis
   C. Zeus
   D. Venus

9. **Arethusa was known for what?**
   A. Magical powers
   B. Musical skills
   C. Speed and agility
   D. Unmatched beauty

10. **Who was Phaethon's father?**
    A. Apollo
    B. Dionysus
    C. Zeus
    D. Cupid

11. **Who killed Phaethon?**
    A. Apollo
    B. Oedipus
    C. Zeus
    D. Bellerophon

12. **What did Apollo promise his son?**
    A. That he would turn into a tree when he died
    B. That he could marry his love
    C. That he would live forever
    D. That he could give him anything he wanted

13. How did Glaucus die?
    A. He killed himself with a knife
    B. He burned in a fire
    C. His horses ate him
    D. Bellerophon killed him while riding Pegasus

14. How did Bellerophon tame Pegasus?
    A. With his enchanting music
    B. With a golden fleece
    C. With his amazing strength
    D. With a golden bridle

15. Why did Proteus want to kill Bellerophon?
    A. To avenge Glaucus's death
    B. Because Bellerophon had tamed Pegasus
    C. Because he thought Bellerophon had tried to seduce his wife
    D. Because Bellerophon had killed his own brother

16. Why did the Lycian king not kill Bellerophon himself?
    A. Because Bellerophon was innocent
    B. Because Bellerophon was immortal
    C. Because Bellerophon had eaten at his table
    D. Because Bellerophon had Pegasus to defend him

17. How did Bellerophon die?
    A. At the hands of the Lycian king
    B. Alone, after he tried to go up to Mount Olympus and Pegasus threw him off his back
    C. Zeus sent a thunderbolt
    D. Chimaera killed him

18. Who did Bellerophon marry?
    A. Artemis
    B. Pegasus
    C. The Lycian queen
    D. Proteus's daughter

19. **How did Otus and Ephialtes die?**
A. Zeus sent a thunderbolt
B. They threw spears at each other
C. They tried to climb Mount Olympus and fell off
D. Poseidon drowned them in a flood

20. **Who did Otus and Ephialtes kidnap?**
A. Hermes
B. Agamemnon
C. Ares
D. Zeus

21. **In their final living moments, what did Otus and Ephialtes try to kill?**
A. Perseus
B. Each other
C. A beautiful white animal
D. Ares

22. **Who designed the Labyrinth?**
A. Icarus
B. Daedalus
C. King Minos
D. Ninus

23. **How did Daedalus build wings?**
A. From wax and feathers
B. With the help of Hermes
C. From a dead eagle
D. With the help of King Minos

24. **Who fell from the sky and died?**
A. Icarus
B. Perseus
C. Daedalus
D. Bellerophon

25. **How did Zeus impregnate Danae when she was carefully guarded?**
    A. The guards fell asleep when Zeus arrived at Danae's door
    B. He came to her in the form of rain
    C. He made himself invisible
    D. He took her across the ocean on the back of a bull

Quiz 2 Answer Key

1. **(B)** That when they die, they die together
2. **(D)** Baucis and Philemon
3. **(A)** Selene
4. **(A)** He will sleep forever
5. **(D)** A laurel tree
6. **(A)** Apollo
7. **(B)** A spring of water
8. **(B)** Artemis
9. **(C)** Speed and agility
10. **(A)** Apollo
11. **(C)** Zeus
12. **(D)** That he could give him anything he wanted
13. **(C)** His horses ate him
14. **(D)** With a golden bridle
15. **(C)** Because he thought Bellerophon had tried to seduce his wife
16. **(C)** Because Bellerophon had eaten at his table
17. **(B)** Alone, after he tried to go up to Mount Olympus and Pegasus threw him off his back
18. **(D)** Proteus's daughter
19. **(B)** They threw spears at each other
20. **(C)** Ares
21. **(C)** A beautiful white animal
22. **(B)** Daedalus
23. **(A)** From wax and feathers
24. **(A)** Icarus
25. **(B)** He came to her in the form of rain

Quiz 3

1. **What god aided Perseus in his fight against Medusa?**
   A. Artemis
   B. Poseidon
   C. Hera
   D. Athena

2. **Why was Andromeda chained to a rock?**
   A. She thought herself better than the gods
   B. As punishment to her foolish mother
   C. As an example to warn King Minos
   D. She was unfaithful

3. **How did Perseus kill his father?**
   A. With a disc
   B. With Medusa's head
   C. With his bare hands
   D. By sinking his ship

4. **How did Aegeus recognize his son?**
   A. By a letter
   B. By his eyes
   C. By the way he spoke
   D. By a sword he had given him

5. **Why was King Minos angry at all of Athens?**
   A. Because Aegeus had killed his son in a match
   B. Because Athenians were of a different race
   C. Because his son had died there
   D. Because Athens was a democracy

6. **Why did Aegeus kill himself?**
   A. Because he saw Theseus's black sail
   B. Because Phaedra gave him false information
   C. Because Theseus died at sea
   D. Because Ariadne died

7. **Who helped Ariadne devise a plan for Theseus's safety?**
    A. Aegeus
    B. Icarus
    C. Daedalus
    D. Minos

8. **Why did Hera send Hercules insanity?**
    A. Because Hercules was Zeus's love child and Hera wanted revenge
    B. Because Hercules thought himself greater than the gods
    C. Because Hercules was not faithful to his wife
    D. Because Hercules was predicted to kill Hera's own son

9. **When did Hercules' strength become obvious?**
    A. As a baby, in the cradle
    B. When he became an adolescent and outran his peers
    C. As he lifted weights as a child
    D. In his mother's womb

10. **Which labor did Hercules NOT undertake?**
    A. Bringing back golden apples
    B. Going to Athens to kill a winged boar
    C. Cleaning thousands of stables
    D. Going to Crete and fetching a bull

11. **Who sent Hercules on his challenges?**
    A. Nephele
    B. Orestes
    C. Melanion
    D. Eurystheus

12. **Who did Atalanta marry?**
    A. Melanion
    B. Medea
    C. Minos
    D. Megara

13. How did Atalanta become a famous huntress?
    A. She killed her father
    B. She killed a wild tiger
    C. She was raised by a she-bear
    D. She killed a ruthless boar

14. What was the first sign of Medea's madness?
    A. She killed Jason's wife
    B. She killed her brother
    C. She lied to Jason
    D. She killed herself

15. What special power did Medea's potion give Jason?
    A. Invisibility
    B. Courage
    C. Invincibility
    D. Strength

16. Who saved Phrixus from his death?
    A. Pelias
    B. Hermes
    C. Nephele
    D. Etes

17. How did Athamus's new wife convince him to kill Phrixus?
    A. She bribed a messenger to say that his sacrifice would end the famine
    B. She threatened she would kill Athamus if he did not kill Phrixus
    C. She threatened she would kill herself if he did not kill Phrixus
    D. She received a message from an oracle

18. From what seeds would a crop of armed men grow?
    A. Athenian blood
    B. Corn seeds
    C. Seeds of fear
    D. Dragon teeth

19. **Whom did Tantalus kill?**
    A. Pelops
    B. King Etes
    C. Penelope
    D. Persephone

20. **Who was Tantalus's father?**
    A. Hercules
    B. Dionysus
    C. Zeus
    D. Atlas

21. **In Hamilton's version of the myth, why was Iphigenia to be killed?**
    A. Because she had killed her brother
    B. Because she had disobeyed her father
    C. Because hunters had killed one of Artemis's favorite wild animals
    D. Because she had thought herself better than the gods

22. **Who intervened on more than one occasion on behalf of Iphigenia?**
    A. Hermes
    B. Hera
    C. Providenza
    D. Athena

23. **Iphigenia's life among the Taurians could be characterized by**
    A. Confusion and apathy
    B. Rage and regret
    C. Loneliness and missing home
    D. Happiness and love

24. **What did Oedipus do when he realized that he had killed his father and married his mother?**
    A. He poked out his eyes
    B. He killed Jocasta
    C. He killed himself
    D. He exiled himself to a cave

25. **What was the correct answer to the Sphinx's riddle to Oedipus?**
    A. Mankind
    B. Animals
    C. Fathers
    D. Babies

Quiz 3 Answer Key

1. **(D)** Athena
2. **(B)** As punishment to her foolish mother
3. **(A)** With a disc
4. **(D)** By a sword he had given him
5. **(C)** Because his son had died there
6. **(A)** Because he saw Theseus's black sail
7. **(C)** Daedalus
8. **(A)** Because Hercules was Zeus's love child and Hera wanted revenge
9. **(A)** As a baby, in the cradle
10. **(B)** Going to Athens to kill a winged boar
11. **(D)** Eurystheus
12. **(A)** Melanion
13. **(D)** She killed a ruthless boar
14. **(B)** She killed her brother
15. **(C)** Invincibility
16. **(B)** Hermes
17. **(A)** She bribed a messenger to say that his sacrifice would end the famine
18. **(D)** Dragon teeth
19. **(A)** Pelops
20. **(C)** Zeus
21. **(C)** Because hunters had killed one of Artemis's favorite wild animals
22. **(D)** Athena
23. **(C)** Loneliness and missing home
24. **(A)** He poked out his eyes
25. **(A)** Mankind

Quiz 4

1. **What did King Laius do to attempt to change the prophecy given to him?**
   A. He put his daughter and her baby out to sea
   B. He left his son on a mountain and assumed him dead
   C. He built a bronze house for his daughter and carefully guarded it
   D. He killed his wife

2. **Who killed Eteocles?**
   A. Ismene
   B. Orestes
   C. Polyneices
   D. Creon

3. **Who did Antigone die for burying?**
   A. Ismene
   B. Oedipus
   C. Eteocles
   D. Polyneices

4. **Who became King of Thebes after Oedipus?**
   A. Orestes
   B. Hercules
   C. Polyneices
   D. Creon

5. **Why must Persephone return to the underworld each year?**
   A. Because she feels obligated
   B. Because she hates her mother
   C. Because she ate the pomegranate seed
   D. Because Hades misses her

6. **Who is Demeter's only daughter?**
   A. Io
   B. Atalanta
   C. Persephone
   D. Niobe

7. **What caused Metaneira to become irate at Demeter?**
    A. Demeter sent the earth into a cold period
    B. Demeter put Metaneira's son in a fire
    C. Demeter made advances on her husband
    D. Demeter ignored her request for immortality

8. **How did Semele die?**
    A. She gave birth to a god
    B. She asked Zeus to show her his glory
    C. She killed herself with shame
    D. She burned in a fire

9. **How did Dionysus kill Penthus?**
    A. By sending a storm to wreck his ship
    B. By turning his followers mad
    C. By gouging out his eyes
    D. By turning his blood into wine

10. **Dionysus rescued his mother and brought her**
    A. Food and water
    B. To Mount Olympus
    C. To Crete to rebuild her kingdom
    D. An endless supply of wine

11. **The Titans were**
    A. Smart and crafty
    B. Malevolent
    C. Large and powerful
    D. Power-crazed

12. **Rhea deceived Cronos by**
    A. Faking a miscarriage
    B. Killing her oldest daughter
    C. Pretending to be asleep
    D. Swallowing a rock instead of Zeus

13. **Zeus punished Atlas by**
    A. Forcing him to hold the weight of the world
    B. Killing all fourteen of his children
    C. Killing him
    D. Never allowing him to eat or drink again

14. **Zeus punished Prometheus by**
    A. Forcing him to hold the weight of the world
    B. Killing his sons and daughters
    C. Tying him to a rock
    D. Exiling him to Crete

15. **Prometheus must endure**
    A. A life without speech
    B. An eagle pecking at his liver
    C. Madness
    D. Water falling constantly on his forehead

16. **Besides giving them fire, what else did Prometheus do to help mankind?**
    A. He gave them emotions
    B. He gave them an upright shape
    C. He gave them ice
    D. He gave them intelligence

17. **Why did Zeus create Pandora?**
    A. To become his mistress
    B. To be a wife for Poseidon
    C. For revenge against Prometheus
    D. To thank Hera

18. **What one positive element came out of Pandora's box?**
    A. Charity
    B. Hope
    C. Love
    D. Forgiveness

19. **Who helped Zeus win the war against the Titans?**
    A. Cronus
    B. Gaea
    C. Niro
    D. Prometheus

20. **Why did Hera turn Io into a heifer?**
    A. Because of a false prophecy
    B. Because Io thought she was greater than the gods
    C. Because Io disrespected her temple
    D. Because she suspected Io's relationship with Zeus

21. **How did Hermes trick Argus?**
    A. With his music
    B. With his riddle
    C. By hiding under his rams
    D. By sneaking out when Argus slept

22. **How did Hera drive Io insane?**
    A. By sending a fly to follow her
    B. By gouging out her eyes
    C. By only allowing her to repeat what others say
    D. By only allowing her to look at food and water, but never eat or drink

23. **What did Europa dream of the night before Zeus came to her?**
    A. Two continents fighting over her
    B. A beautiful bull
    C. Eating her own children
    D. Zeus himself

24. **How did Zeus first come to Europa?**
    A. As a lamb
    B. As a baby
    C. As a bull
    D. As a musician

25. Why did Zeus fall in love with Europa?

A. Because she tantalized him
B. Because Cupid hit him with an arrow
C. Because she was the most beautiful woman on earth
D. Because he wanted to have a child

Quiz 4 Answer Key

1. (**B**) He left his son on a mountain and assumed him dead
2. (**C**) Polyneices
3. (**D**) Polyneices
4. (**D**) Creon
5. (**C**) Because she ate the pomegranate seed
6. (**C**) Persephone
7. (**B**) Demeter put Metaneira's son in a fire
8. (**B**) She asked Zeus to show her his glory
9. (**B**) By turning his followers mad
10. (**B**) To Mount Olympus
11. (**C**) Large and powerful
12. (**D**) Swallowing a rock instead of Zeus
13. (**A**) Forcing him to hold the weight of the world
14. (**C**) Tying him to a rock
15. (**B**) An eagle pecking at his liver
16. (**B**) He gave them an upright shape
17. (**C**) For revenge against Prometheus
18. (**B**) Hope
19. (**D**) Prometheus
20. (**D**) Because she suspected Io's relationship with Zeus
21. (**A**) With his music
22. (**A**) By sending a fly to follow her
23. (**A**) Two continents fighting over her
24. (**C**) As a bull
25. (**B**) Because Cupid hit him with an arrow

ClassicNotes

GradeSaver™

Getting you the grade since 1999™

Other ClassicNotes from GradeSaver™

12 Angry Men
1984
A&P and Other Stories
Absalom, Absalom
Adam Bede
The Adventures of Augie
    March
The Adventures of
    Huckleberry Finn
The Adventures of Tom
    Sawyer
The Aeneid
Agamemnon
The Age of Innocence
The Alchemist (Coelho)
The Alchemist (Jonson)
Alice in Wonderland
All My Sons
All Quiet on the Western
    Front
All the King's Men
All the Pretty Horses
Allen Ginsberg's Poetry
The Ambassadors
American Beauty
Amusing Ourselves to
    Death
The Analects of
    Confucius
And Then There Were
    None
Angela's Ashes
Animal Farm
Anna Karenina
Anthem
Antigone

Antony and Cleopatra
Aristotle's Poetics
Aristotle's Politics
Aristotle: Nicomachean
    Ethics
As I Lay Dying
As You Like It
Astrophil and Stella
Atlas Shrugged
Atonement
The Awakening
Babbitt
The Bacchae
Bartleby the Scrivener
The Bean Trees
The Bell Jar
Beloved
Benito Cereno
Beowulf
Bhagavad-Gita
Billy Budd
The Birthday Party
Black Boy
Bleak House
Bless Me, Ultima
Blindness
Blood Meridian: Or the
    Evening Redness in
    the West
Blood Wedding
The Bloody Chamber
Bluest Eye
The Bonfire of the
    Vanities
The Book of Daniel

The Book of the Duchess
    and Other Poems
The Book Thief
Brave New World
Breakfast at Tiffany's
Breakfast of Champions
The Brief Wondrous Life
    of Oscar Wao
The Brothers Karamazov
The Burning Plain and
    Other Stories
A Burnt-Out Case
By Night in Chile
Call of the Wild
Candide
The Canterbury Tales
Cat on a Hot Tin Roof
Cat's Cradle
Catch-22
The Catcher in the Rye
Cathedral
The Caucasian Chalk
    Circle
Charlotte Temple
Charlotte's Web
The Cherry Orchard
The Chocolate War
The Chosen
A Christmas Carol
Christopher Marlowe's
    Poems
Chronicle of a Death
    Foretold
Civil Disobedience
Civilization and Its
    Discontents

For our full list of over 250 Study Guides, Quizzes,
Sample College Application Essays, Literature Essays and E-texts, visit:

www.gradesaver.com

ClassicNotes

Getting you the grade since 1999™

ClassicNotes

GradeSaver™
Getting you the grade since 1999™

Other ClassicNotes from GradeSaver™

Gulliver's Travels
Hamlet
The Handmaid's Tale
Hard Times
Haroun and the Sea of
    Stories
Harry Potter and the
    Philosopher's Stone
Heart of Darkness
Hedda Gabler
Henry IV (Pirandello)
Henry IV Part 1
Henry IV Part 2
Henry V
Herzog
Hippolytus
The History of Tom
    Jones, a Foundling
The Hobbit
Homo Faber
The House of Bernarda
    Alba
House of Mirth
The House of the Seven
    Gables
The House of the Spirits
House on Mango Street
How the Garcia Girls
    Lost Their Accents
Howards End
A Hunger Artist
The Hunger Games
I Know Why the Caged
    Bird Sings
I, Claudius
An Ideal Husband

Iliad
The Importance of Being
    Earnest
In Cold Blood
In Our Time
In the Skin of a Lion
In the Time of the
    Butterflies
Incidents in the Life of a
    Slave Girl
Inherit the Wind
An Inspector Calls
Interpreter of Maladies
Into the Wild
Invisible Man
The Island of Dr. Moreau
Jane Eyre
Jazz
The Jew of Malta
Johnny Tremain
Joseph Andrews
A Journal of the Plague
    Year
The Joy Luck Club
Jude the Obscure
Julius Caesar
The Jungle
Jungle of Cities
Kama Sutra
Kate Chopin's Short
    Stories
Kidnapped
King Lear
King Solomon's Mines
The Kite Runner

The Lais of Marie de
    France
Lancelot: Or, the Knight
    of the Cart
Last of the Mohicans
Le Morte d'Arthur
Leaves of Grass
Legend
The Legend of Sleepy
    Hollow
A Lesson Before Dying
Leviathan
Libation Bearers
Life is Beautiful
The Life of Olaudah
    Equiano
Life of Pi
Light In August
Like Water for Chocolate
The Lion, the Witch and
    the Wardrobe
Little Women
Lolita
Long Day's Journey Into
    Night
A Long Way Gone
Look Back in Anger
Lord Byron's Poems
Lord Jim
Lord of the Flies
The Lord of the Rings:
    The Fellowship of the
    Ring
The Lord of the Rings:
    The Return of the
    King

For our full list of over 250 Study Guides, Quizzes,
Sample College Application Essays, Literature Essays and E-texts, visit:

www.gradesaver.com

ClassicNotes

GradeSaver™

Getting you the grade since 1999™

Other ClassicNotes from GradeSaver™

The Lord of the Rings: The Two Towers
A Lost Lady
The Lottery and Other Stories
Love in the Time of Cholera
The Love Song of J. Alfred Prufrock
The Lovely Bones
Lucy
Macbeth
Madame Bovary
Maestro
Maggie: A Girl of the Streets and Other Stories
Manhattan Transfer
Mankind: Medieval Morality Plays
Mansfield Park
The Marrow of Tradition
The Master and Margarita
MAUS
The Mayor of Casterbridge
The Maze Runner
Measure for Measure
Medea
Merchant of Venice
Metamorphoses
The Metamorphosis
Midaq Alley
Middlemarch
Middlesex

A Midsummer Night's Dream
The Mill on the Floss
Moby Dick
A Modest Proposal and Other Satires
Moll Flanders
The Most Dangerous Game
Mother Courage and Her Children
Mrs. Dalloway
Much Ado About Nothing
Murder in the Cathedral
My Antonia
Mythology
The Namesake
The Narrative of Arthur Gordon Pym of Nantucket
Narrative of the Life of Frederick Douglass
Native Son
Nervous Conditions
Never Let Me Go
Nickel and Dimed: On (Not) Getting By in America
Night
Nine Stories
No Exit
North and South
Northanger Abbey
Notes from Underground
O Pioneers

The Odyssey
Oedipus Rex or Oedipus the King
Of Mice and Men
The Old Man and the Sea
Oliver Twist
On Liberty
On the Road
One Day in the Life of Ivan Denisovich
One Flew Over the Cuckoo's Nest
One Hundred Years of Solitude
Oroonoko
Oryx and Crake
Othello
Our Town
The Outsiders
Pale Fire
Pamela: Or Virtue Rewarded
Paradise Lost
A Passage to India
The Pearl
Pedro Paramo
Percy Shelley: Poems
Perfume: The Story of a Murderer
Persepolis: The Story of a Childhood
Persuasion
Phaedra
Phaedrus
The Piano Lesson

For our full list of over 250 Study Guides, Quizzes,
Sample College Application Essays, Literature Essays and E-texts, visit:

www.gradesaver.com

ClassicNotes

Getting you the grade since 1999™

Other ClassicNotes from GradeSaver™

The Picture of Dorian
  Gray
Pilgrim's Progress
Poe's Poetry
Poe's Short Stories
Poems of W.B. Yeats:
  The Rose
Poems of W.B. Yeats:
  The Tower
The Poems of William
  Blake
The Poisonwood Bible
Pope's Poems and Prose
Portrait of the Artist as a
  Young Man
The Praise of Folly
Pride and Prejudice
The Prince
The Professor's House
Prometheus Bound
Pudd'nhead Wilson
Purple Hibiscus
Pygmalion
Rabbit, Run
A Raisin in the Sun
The Real Life of
  Sebastian Knight
Rebecca
The Red Badge of
  Courage
The Remains of the Day
The Republic
Return of the Native
Rhinoceros
Richard II
Richard III

The Rime of the Ancient
  Mariner
Rip Van Winkle and
  Other Stories
The Road
Robert Browning: Poems
Robert Frost: Poems
Robinson Crusoe
Roll of Thunder, Hear
  My Cry
Romeo and Juliet
A Room of One's Own
A Room With a View
A Rose For Emily and
  Other Short Stories
Rosencrantz and
  Guildenstern Are
  Dead
Rudyard Kipling: Poems
Salome
The Satanic Verses
The Scarlet Letter
The Scarlet Pimpernel
Schindler's List
The Seagull
Season of Migration to
  the North
Second Treatise of
  Government
The Secret Life of Bees
The Secret River
Secret Sharer
Sense and Sensibility
A Separate Peace
Shakespeare's Sonnets
Shantaram

She Stoops to Conquer
Short Stories of Ernest
  Hemingway
Short Stories of F. Scott
  Fitzgerald
Siddhartha
Silas Marner
Sir Gawain and the
  Green Knight
Sir Thomas Wyatt:
  Poems
Sister Carrie
Six Characters in Search
  of an Author
Slaughterhouse Five
Snow Falling on Cedars
The Social Contract
Something Wicked This
  Way Comes
Song of Roland
Song of Solomon
Songs of Innocence and
  of Experience
Sons and Lovers
The Sorrows of Young
  Werther
The Sound and the Fury
The Sound of Waves
The Spanish Tragedy
Speak
Spenser's Amoretti and
  Epithalamion
Spring Awakening
The Stranger
A Streetcar Named
  Desire

For our full list of over 250 Study Guides, Quizzes,
Sample College Application Essays, Literature Essays and E-texts, visit:

www.gradesaver.com

Made in the USA
San Bernardino, CA
02 September 2013